DYNAMICALLY ORIENTED ART THERAPY:
Its Principles and Practices

Illustrated with Three Case Studies

by MARGARET NAUMBURG

Magnolia Street Publishers   **Chicago**

1987 Published by

MAGNOLIA STREET PUBLISHERS
1250 W. Victoria
Chicago, Illinois 60660

ISBN: 0-9613309-1-0
Library of Congress Catalog Card No. 87-042989
Cover Design: Sarah Reinken
Printed in the USA

CONTENTS

INTRODUCTION

    I. Art Therapy: Basic Review and Definition...................... 1
   II. Questions about Dynamically Oriented Art Therapy............ 4
  III. How Dynamically Oriented Art Therapy Differs from Other
        Psychotherapeutic Approaches 16
   IV. How Dynamically Oriented Art Therapy Evolved............... 30
    V. Development of Dynamically Oriented Art Therapy in the
        United States 31
   VI. The Power of the Symbol in Dynamically Oriented Art Therapy.... 36

FOREWORD to Three Case Studies Illustrating the Theory and Practice of
        Dynamically Oriented Art Therapy.......................... 48
    I. ART THERAPY IN THE TREATMENT OF AN ULCER
        PATIENT, A PROFESSIONAL ARTIST...................... 49
   II. IMAGES AND HALLUCINATIONS OF AN
        ALCOHOLIC PATIENT.................................... 85
  III. ART THERAPY IN THE TREATMENT OF A
        DEPRESSED WOMAN.................................... 129

INDEX 167

ILLUSTRATIONS

I. ART THERAPY IN THE TREATMENT OF AN ULCER PATIENT,
   A PROFESSIONAL ARTIST
       1. "Myself Surrounded by Ice": from a Dream................ 54
       2. "Odalisque: Myself as a Glamorous Female.".............. 55
       3. Broken Tree: a Dream................................... 57
       4. The Phallic Mother: Based on an Earlier Dream........... 58
          Color plate on page x.
    5a., 5b. Two Pencil Doodles of Mother and Child (The first
         transference images) 59
       6. Abstract Design (Scribble).............................. 61
       7. "Devil": an Unconscious Symbol of the "Bad" Mother
         (Scribble) 61
       8. Double Fetal Form (Scribble)............................ 62
      9a. First Dream: the Bull Represents the Sexual Threat
         of the Father 63

v

9b. Second Dream: The Bull, as Father, Is Being Appeased
with Silver Paper Packages by the Patient.................. 65

10. Mouth with Teeth and Tongue: as Symbol of Oral
Regression (Scribble) 67

11. A Puppy Dog with a Bone: Threatened by a Claw-like
Hand of the Mother (Elaborated from a doodle)............ 68

12a., 12b. Two Puppy Doodles 69

13. The Mother Wolf and the Suckling Child (Begun as a scribble) 70

14. Green Skull and Predatory Hands: an Unconscious Death
Wish against the Father................................. 73
Color plate on page xi.

15. "Now the Cat Is out of the Bag.".......................... 73
Color plate on page xi.

16. "Green Elephant and Grey Shark, Combined with Black Square
of Depression and Orange Core of Hope" (Scribble)........ 75

17. Mouth with Tongue....................................... 76

18. "A Green Frog-like Creature Representing Myself:
an Expression of Sexual Confusion in Childhood.".......... 77

19. "Myself Running Away" (Scribble)........................ 78

20. "The Patient as a Pleading Child behind Her Parents"
(Doodle) 80

21. Hermaphrodite Form: Representing Masculine and Feminine
Aspects of the Patient (Doodle)......................... 81

22. "A Doodle, Begun as a Woman, Turns into a Man.".......... 82

23. Male Figure Symbolizing the Ambivalence of the Patient
(Doodle) 82

24. Another Mother Portrait: Projection of the Patient's
Unconscious Hostility against the Mother.................. 83
Color plate on page x.

II. IMAGES AND HALLUCINATIONS OF AN ALCOHOLIC PATIENT

25. First Monster Drawing: the Patient's Struggle
with the Monster.. 88

26. The Green Monster and Huge Breast...................... 88

27. Figure of the Patient with the Monster Chained below....... 90

28. "Bright Colors in the Center of a Dark Picture: It's a Ray of
Light and Hope Working with M.N.".................... 92
Color plate on page xii.

29. "I Am Clinging to the Cliff While the Sun Looks Down at Me
with a Mocking Smile.".................................. 92
Color plate on page xii.

30. The Dead Mother and the Black Coffin.................... 92
Color plate on page xiii.

31. The Patient Kneels Beside an Explosion: and as a Child Is
Being Pinched in the Stomach by Her Brother.............. 94

32. "Figure of Myself on a Stage: The Audience Is Dr. G.,
    You and Myself.".. 102
33. "My Two Selves in a Circus: My Tight-rope Picture.".......... 102
34. "The Graveyard, Two Men and a Young Girl.".............. 104
35. "My Brother's Hand.".................................... 105
36. "The Red Stocking and the Mouse.".................... 105
    Color plate on page xiii.
37. The Patient as a Baby on Her Doctor's Lap................. 107
    Color plate on page xiv.
38. "Pig with Its Throat Cut, Spurting Blood.".................. 108
39. "Myself As a Child in Bed with a Pig Monster: a Dream.".... 109
40. One Black Monster Drawing............................. 109
41a. "Myself with a Rope Around Me" (First scribble drawing).. 111
41b. "Dr. G and Me" (Scribble)............................... 111
42. "Memory of Myself Visiting Mother in an Insane Asylum.".... 112
    Color plate on page xv.
43. "Things in Me That Want To Be Wretched and Rot.".......... 112
    Color plate on page xiv.
44. Development of the "My Universe" Picture: First Version.... 115
    Color plate on page xv.
45. Another Pencil Drawing for the "Universe" Picture.......... 116
46. "The Black Elm Tree": Subtitled "My Universe Now."....... 119
47. "My Rock with Vulture and M.N.'s Reflected Universe."....... 119
    Color plate on page xvii.
48. "M.N. Is Dancing with a Tree: and I am in the pool, Holding
    to Her Reflected Universe.".............................. 120
    Color plate on page xviii.
49. "An Empty Couch.".. 120
50. "My Older Brother Doing the Doctor Jekyll and Mr. Hyde
    Business." 121
51. "On the Couch.".. 122
52. "On the Couch Again.".................................... 122
53. "Four Corpses in a Hospital": a Dream..................... 123
54. Young Woman Carrying Two Pails......................... 124
55. "My Conscience." 124
    Color plate on page xvi.
56. "Join the Maypole Dance.".............................. 126
57. Flowers with Black Centers............................. 133
58. The Upright Plate of Fruit............................. 135
59. Abstract Blue Pattern.................................. 137
60. Bloody Hands 138
61. Three Black Tombstones................................ 139
62. A Second Picture of the Black Tombstones and Black Trees,
    Brightened with Rust-Colored Blossoms.................. 140
63. Black Jar with Yellow Flower........................... 141
64. The Patient Mourning with a Red Rose at the Tomstones of
    Her Dead Family... 143

III. ART THERAPY IN THE TREATMENT OF A DEPRESSED WOMAN

    65. A Phantasied Self-Portrait.............................. 144
    66. "A Pregnant Woman."................................... 145
    67. Pewter Picture with Autumn Leaves and Grapes........... 146
    68. A Blue Table and Fruit................................. 147
    69. Self-Image with Black Surround and Flower Spray.......... 148
    70. Vase of Gladiolas on a Stand........................... 149
    71. "Woman in a Golden Dress": First Dream................. 151
    72. "My Husband's Hand Reaching Down from Icy Mountains,
        and My Own Hand, Unable to Get Him": Second Dream.... 152
    73. "A Mermaid." 153
        Color plate on page xx.
    74. "A Woman and a Tree: Eternity for Me.".................. 155
    75. "Four Generations: Eternity and Sufferings.".............. 157
        Color plate on page xxiv.
    76. "The Dream of My Blue Evening Dress": Made after Seeing
        the Play "The Rose Tattoo.".............................. 157
        Color plate on page xix.
    77. "The Hat: My Feelings about My Sister.".................. 159
        Color plate on page xxi.
    78. "Myself, My Children and My Grandchild.".............. 159
        Color plate on page xxii.
    79. "Myself as a Child: My Father and Myself Grown Up.".... 161
        Color plate on page xxiii.
    80. "Myself with All the Men Staring at Me.".................. 163
    81. Bowl of Peonies... 164

Dynamically Oriented Art Therapy
Color Plates

Fig. 24.   **Another Mother Portrait: Projection of the Patient's Unconscious Hostility against the Mother.** Original drawing 17¾″ x 23¾″.

Fig. 4.   **The Phallic Mother: Based on an Earlier Dream.** Original drawing 8¾″ x 11¾″.

Fig. 14. **Green Skull and Predatory Hands: an Unconscious Death Wish against the Father.** Original drawing 23¾ x 18⅝".

Fig. 15. **"Now the Cat is out of the Bag."** Original drawing 23¾" x 18⅝".

Fig. 28. "Bright Colors in the Center of a Dark Picture: It's a Ray of Light and Hope Working with M.N." Original drawing 16⅝″ x 13¾″.

Fig. 29. "I am Clinging to the Cliff While the Sun Looks Down at Me with a Mocking Smile." Original drawing 16⅝″ x 13¾″.

Fig. 30. The Dead Mother and the Black Coffin. Original drawing 16⅝" x 13¾".

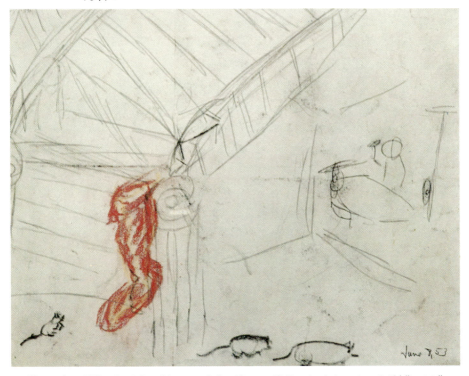

Fig. 36. "The Red Stocking and the Mouse." Original drawing 14¾" x 12".

Fig. 37.   **The Patient as a Baby on Her Doctor's Lap.** Original drawing
16⅝″ x 13¾″.

Fig. 43.   **"Things in Me That Want to Be Wretched and Rot."** Original
drawing 16⅝″ x 13¾″.

Fig. 42. "Memory of Myself Visiting Mother in an Insane Asylum."
Original drawing 25½″ x 18⅝″.

Fig. 44. Development of the "My Universe" Picture: First Version.
Original drawing 16½″ x 13¾″.

Fig. 55. "My Conscience." Original drawing 11¾″ x 17¾″.

Fig. 47. "My Rock with Vulture and M.N.'s Reflected Universe." Original
drawing 17¼" x 23¼".

Fig. 48. "M.N. Is Dancing with a Tree: and I am in the Pool, Holding to Her Reflected Universe." Original drawing 16¾″ x 22¼″.

Fig. 76. "The Dream of My Blue Evening Dress": Made after Seeing the Play "The Rose Tattoo." Original drawing 18¾" x 23¾".

Fig. 73.   "A Mermaid." Original drawing 18¾" x 23¾".

Fig. 77. "The Hat: My Feelings about My Sister." Original drawing 18¾" x 23¾".

Fig. 78. "Myself, My Children and My Grandchild." Original drawing 18⅝″ x 24″.

Fig. 79.   "Myself as a Child: My Father and Myself Grown Up." Original
drawing 18⅝" x 24".

Fig. 75. "Four Generations: Eternity and Suffering." Original drawing 18¾" x 23¾".

INTRODUCTION

I. ART THERAPY: BASIC REVIEW AND DEFINITION

Dynamically oriented art therapy has been an established form of psychotherapy for over 26 years, and it continues to gain recognition and support from psychiatrists and psychoanalysts. The procedures of art therapy as a distinctive form of psychotherapy have received response not only from the medical profession, but also from psychologists, art educators, occupational therapists, social workers and those in special education—all of whom have found in it useful aspects which will be discussed later.

Nature and Purpose

The process of dynamically oriented art therapy is based on the recognition that man's fundamental thoughts and feelings are derived from the unconscious and often reach expression in images rather than in words. By means of pictorial projection, art therapy encourages a method of symbolic communication between patient and therapist. Its images may, as in psychoanalytic procedures, also deal with the data of dreams, phantasies, daydreams, fears, conflicts and childhood memories. The techniques of art therapy are based on the knowledge that every individual, whether trained or untrained in art, has a latent capacity to project his inner conflicts into visual form. As patients picture such inner experiences, they frequently become more verbally articulate. Through the use of graphic or plastic expression, those who originally blocked in speech often begin to verbalize in order to explain their art productions.

Art therapy accepts as basic to its treatment methods the psychoanalytic approach to the mechanisms of repression, projection, identification, sublimation and condensation. In dynamically oriented art therapy a patient's spontaneous visual projections and unconscious responses are frequently expressed more directly in pictures than in words. In psychoanalytic treatment the patient is encouraged to use free association in order to express his thoughts and feelings

1

in words, while in art therapy the process of free association is applied, as well, to the spontaneous art projected by each patient.

In art therapy the patient's unconscious imaged experience (of dream or phantasy) is transposed directly into an actual pictured image. In psychoanalytic treatment such inner visual experiences must be retranslated from an imaged into a verbal communication. Freud has referred to this subject in the following way:

> "We experience it [a dream] predominantly in visual images; feelings may be present too, and thoughts interwoven in it as well; the other senses may also experience something, but nonetheless it is predominantly a question of images. Part of the difficulty of giving an account of dreams is due to our having to translate these images into words. 'I could draw it,' a dreamer often says to us, 'but I don't know how to say it.' "[1]

Although Freud made the modern world aware that the unconscious speaks in images, he did not follow the suggestion of his patients that they be permitted to draw their dreams rather than to tell them. Art therapy, however, encourages just such an expression of inner experience. Objectified picturization acts then as an immediate symbolic communication which frequently circumvents the difficulties of speech. Another advantage inherent in the making of unconscious pictured projections is that such symbolic images more easily escape repression by what Freud called the mind's "censor" than do verbal expressions, which are more familiar to the patient.

By projecting interior images into exteriorized designs, art therapy crystallizes and fixes in lasting form the recollections of dreams or phantasies which would otherwise remain evanescent and might quickly be forgotten. It is usable for adults, adolescents or children, and for persons with behavior disorders as well as for neurotic and psychotic patients.

Dynamically oriented art therapy was originally applied to the treatment of individual patients, but it is now also being used as a supplementary technique in various forms of psychiatric group therapy.

The art therapist does not interpret the symbolic art expression of his patient, but encourages the patient to discover for himself the meaning of his art productions. Even if a patient does not at first understand what his series of symbolic designs means to him, it is possible, by the use of free association and recovery of the moods or circumstances under which the designs were made, to help him to uncover their inner meaning.

In art therapy, as in psychoanalysis, the patient's capacity to verify the significance of his symbolic expression always takes place in a transference relation. When the therapist convinces the patient that he accepts whatever the patient may express, the patient often begins to project in images what he dares not put into words. If this happens, the patient is faced with evidence of a concretized image of his conflict released from the unconscious by his drawing,

---

[1] Freud, S.: *New Introductory Lectures on Psychoanalysis* (Ed. James Strachey). Part II: "Dreams." London, The Hogarth Press, 1963, Vol. XV, p. 90.

painting or sculpture. When a forbidden impulse has found such form outside the patient's psyche, he gains a detachment from his conflict which often enables him to examine his problems with growing objectivity. Thus a patient is gradually assisted to recognize that his artistic productions can be treated as a mirror in which he can begin to find his own motives revealed. The autonomy of the patient is encouraged by his growing ability to contribute to the verbal interpretation of his own art productions. Whereas he originally depended on the therapist, he gradually substitutes a narcissistic cathexis to his own art to his previous dependence on the therapist.

The patient is gradually freed from overdependence on the therapist, who withholds interpretation and thereby encourages the patient to discover for himself what his symbolic pictures mean to him. Like the professional artist, the patient develops a narcissistic identification with his own creations. It is interesting to note that patients unfamiliar with other forms of psychotherapy sometimes associate to their symbolic productions in ways that confirm either a Freudian or Jungian interpretation of symbols. (In the section on *Symbolism*, this matter will be considered more fully.)

Psychoanalysts are well aware of the symbolic significance of various types of nonverbal communication offered by their patients—such as gesture, posture, tone of voice and facial expression—but many of these analysts do not as yet seem to recognize the significance and value of spontaneous art projection as a useful form of nonverbal communication. Since our culture is primarily verbal, it is understandable, however, that most academic and professional training has emphasized verbal forms of communication. This may explain why it has been difficult for some psychiatrists and psychoanalysts to recognize the promise that the creation of spontaneous images has to offer as a means of frequently projecting the unconscious conflicts of patients into pictures before they are able to describe them in words. Psychoanalysts sometimes forget that it was Freud who first emphasized that the unconscious speaks in images in our dreams. Art therapy recognizes that the unconscious as expressed in a patient's phantasies, daydreams and fears can be projected more immediately in pictures than in words. That is why art therapy is frequently effective as a method of treatment. (Examples of how the unconscious projection of pictures leads, through free association, to the release of long-repressed conflicts are shown in the three case histories in this book.)

Not so long ago I met a well-known psychoanalyst, a director of a leading psychoanalytic training institute, who asked me to explain to him the basic concepts of art therapy. I spoke of how the projection of dreams, phantasies and daydreams into spontaneous images could be more direct expression than words, and reminded him that Freud's own patients had told him that they often could not tell him their dreams but could draw them. The analyst replied, "Why bother with making pictures, as they will have to be put into words anyway?" Like some other psychoanalysts anchored in verbalization as the only mode of treatment, he did not realize that the spontaneous creation in art therapy leads to a speeding up of verbalization. Art therapy is not opposed to verbalization, which it too uses in combination with spontaneous art production, but it has been shown that patients become able to associate freely in words to the spontaneous images that they have created, and this leads inevitably to a speeding up of the therapeutic process.

II. QUESTIONS ABOUT DYNAMICALLY ORIENTED ART THERAPY

Many questions are asked about the nature and purpose of art therapy, so an attempt will be made to answer them in a direct and systematic way under specific headings.

What Brings People to Art Therapy?

There appear to be two main types of individuals who seek art therapy, but each type has different motivations. One type consists of those whose neuroses are blocking their creative expression. [The first case in this book (an ulcer patient who was a professional artist unable to paint for six years) is a case of this kind.]

A larger group of neurotic individuals seek treatment by means of art therapy in the hope that it will help to release their latent creative talent, as well as help them therapeutically. [The second case in this book (an alcoholic woman), as well as the third case (a depressed woman), illustrate this type of motivation.] Both patients sought help through dynamically oriented art therapy in order to resolve their problems and gain help in the development of their creative expression. There are others, however, who are unhappy and insecure and simply want help to find themselves.

Treatment of a professional artist by means of dynamically oriented art therapy involves a special type of difficulty. Because he has been professionally trained in the use of form and color, he unconsciously resists any attempt to have him release his repressions in spontaneous imagery. At first he tends to draw entirely conscious designs which are technically knowledgeable but without significance as a release of unconscious conflicts. When, however, such an artist succeeds in creating his first truly spontaneous image, he is usually eager to develop it into an artistically finished picture. He must then be made to understand that, in order to deal with his unconscious motivation, such imagery must be regarded as a form of symbolic speech to which he must learn to make free association. The artist is told that when his therapy has been completed he will be free to use his spontaneous pictures in any way he chooses.

The spontaneous art projections of many who are untrained in art serve primarily as an immediate way of releasing unconscious conflicts and have little esthetic significance, yet a number of patients without previous art training have succeeded in developing capacities of genuine artistic expression.[2] Such occurrences continue to be a source of surprise to both professional artists and those art critics who are convinced that the creation of significant art depends on adequate art training.

----

[2] For illustrations of this point, see Naumburg, Margaret: *Psychoneurotic Art: Its Use in Psychotherapy*. New York, Grune & Stratton, 1963.

Art therapy has shown that with the release of the distortions caused by repression, the spontaneous art of many untrained individuals becomes vivid and original. (The changes that took place in the expression of the alcoholic and the depressed patients described in this book offer dramatic evidence of how beautiful drawings and paintings can evolve as conflicts are being resolved.)

Many of the patients who sought aid through psychotherapy were originally unaware of this new approach of dynamically oriented art therapy. While some of these patients seemed satisfied with an entirely verbal method of therapy, others became interested in the possibilities of the art therapy approach when it was introduced to them and responded enthusiastically to the opportunities it offered. There have been patients who, while preferring a verbal form of communication, would resort at certain crises in their lives to creating spontaneous and significant pictures.

At times, patients who have done no drawing or painting during art therapy may, when beginning to face a crisis in their lives, suddenly express it in a picture. An example of this occurred in the case of a young engineer who found he had lost his sense of direction on returning to civilian life after his army service. As he began to recall his earlier years and his uncertainty about the profession he had previously chosen, he suddenly drew a picture which symbolized his entire life. The picture showed three paths: the one on the left dramatized an episode of childhood happiness with the patient sailing a toy boat in the center of the picture. The second path was a mingling of dark colors which, he explained, showed the turbulence he felt about his present profession, since he now doubted that he was fitted to pursue it. He said that the third path, drawn at the right, was incomplete in order to express the uncertainty that he felt about the future direction of his life. The two years of psychotherapy which followed this drawing were dealt with primarily on the verbal level. Only in the final sessions did this young man choose to end his therapy with the drawing of two abstract geometric forms: a sphere and octahedron which he said expressed symbolically his sense of unification in the form of his present and future life.

It must not be forgotten that the effectiveness of the art therapy approach does not depend on a recognized artistic capacity, even though many artistically gifted patients, when blocked in their creative expression, have been helped through art therapy to recover their creative powers. A latent creative capacity exists in every human being, whatever the apparent artistic gift or lack of creative ability shown at first by patients in art therapy. But in order to help the release of many forms of spontaneous art through dynamically oriented art therapy, students require special training to become able therapists, who not only understand the process of art therapy but can also employ its special techniques in a competent and understanding way.

A number of significant case studies showing art therapy treatment of patients with different needs have been presented at two symposia at the annual meetings of the Orthopsychiatric Association. Unfortunately, they have not yet been published. Among these studies were two papers by Dr. Ralph Rabinovitch, Director of the Psychiatric Children's Hospital, Hawthorne Center, North-ville, Michigan. In both papers he showed that many types of disturbed children under his care could be treated successfully by means of art therapy. It should also be mentioned that Dr. Rabinovitch, besides employing dynamically oriented art therapy in his personal treatment of a number of the children in his hospital, has also trained his entire staff—interns, psychologists, teachers and social workers —in the methods of using art therapy in treatment.

For Whom Is Dynamically Oriented Art Therapy Suitable?

In terms of my own experience and that of many others in the professions of psychiatry, psychoanalysis, psychology and especially art therapy, a wide range of neurotic and psychotic adult patients, as well as emotionally disturbed adolescents and children, has been treated successfully by means of dynamically oriented art therapy. These various types of patients have been treated in private practice, psychiatric hospitals and clinics. Adolescents and children have some-times been cared for in special schools where dynamically trained art therapists have worked in conjunction with psychiatrists.

How Is Art Therapy Carried Out?

When spontaneous images are created by a patient in art therapy, the therapist encourages the patient to give his free associations to the image that he makes. Unlike the psychoanalyst, the art therapist does not interpret a pa-tient's imaged projections but encourages the patient to assume the active role of explaining his creations. The entire process of discovering the meaning of his symbolic art takes place within the framework of the established transfer-ence to the therapist. Even when a patient does not understand the meaning of his symbolic art projections, the art therapist, although grasping the meaning of a picture, does not then offer him an interpretation but waits until other pic-tures are brought by the patient to another session. After some of his problems have been verbalized, the patient then becomes able to evoke free associations to his new pictures and finds it possible to clarify the meaning of pictures which had until that time eluded him. Sometimes, however, when a patient says that he does not understand his pictures, he is suddenly able to realize their meaning in the presence of the therapist. A therapist's questions as to the mood in which the patient's designs were created, or the order in which the colors were used, or just what the pictures meant to the patient may release his free associations. These questions may suddenly reveal to the patient the symbolic significance of his picture.

When the art therapist convinces a patient that whatever spontaneous images he releases from the unconscious are to be considered as a form of sym-bolic speech rather than as works of art, it helps the patient to become more relaxed. When the patient is convinced that the therapist accepts, without esthetic judgment, whatever he releases from his unconscious, the patient is relieved and is then able to create images which escape the denial of the Freudian "censor" in a way that words cannot. A picture often speaks symboli-cally before the patient understands its meaning—a frequent occurrence when a forbidden impulse is exteriorized into some momentarily unrecognizable visual symbols in a picture. The patient thus discovers, as he associates freely to the different aspects of his design, that he has projected symbolically an image which tells of a repressed conflict or an unspoken anxiety. When a patient begins to understand how a repressed impulse can escape repression by the "censor" through an imaged projection, he gains increased detachment and greater insight. He thus comes to understand, through his growing recognition of the symbolic significance of his spontaneous art expression, that his pictures can be regarded as a kind of mirror which reflects, through his free associations, what is taking place in his unconscious.

Does Art Therapy Prevent Verbalization?

This question has been asked by certain psychoanalysts who regard verbalization as the essential means of psychotherapy. The writer's own experience has shown that a number of patients who at the beginning of art therapy treatment were blocked in speech could, after creating images of dreams and phantasies, make free associations to their pictures and become more verbally fluent during art therapy. Confirmation of this was once again received in a recent letter from a woman who had just completed three years of art therapy with the author. She wrote, "If I hadn't been able to begin by making pictures about my problems, I would never have been able to speak about them so freely later on." Art therapists have found that the art therapy approach, instead of inhibiting verbalization, tends to expand each patient's power of expression in both words and pictures.

When Do Patients Create Their Spontaneous Art?

Patients treated by means of art therapy are left free to choose whether to create their spontaneous images during art therapy sessions in the presence of the therapist or whether to make them by themselves at home or on a hospital ward. Also, there are some patients who sometimes draw and paint in the presence of the therapist and at other times create their pictures at home. (In the case studies of the three women described in this book, each one created most of her pictures at home and then brought them to the therapy sessions in order to discover or discuss their symbolic significance with the art therapist.)

When and How is Spontaneous Art Expression Introduced to Patients?

The extent to which spontaneous art is produced by patients in the course of art therapy varies greatly. Some patients who find it easier to express themselves in pictures than in words create pictures and sometimes sculpture throughout the therapy sessions. Other patients may begin by creating many spontaneous pictures and then, as their verbalization becomes more fluent, cease making any pictures. As in the case of the young man who created a picture only at a crisis in his life, the decision is left to a patient to choose to what extent he wishes to project images of his dreams, phantasies, conflicts and wishes in the course of therapy.

The length of time needed for sessions in art therapy varies with different patients. While the "50-minute hour" may be used at the beginning of art therapy, this must frequently be lengthened to an hour and a half if the patient needs more time to create drawings or paintings in the presence of the art therapist. The frequency of appointments for art therapy sessions usually ranges from three times to once a week, but under special circumstances, particularly if patients must travel long distances (as in the first case of the ulcer patient in this book), the art therapy periods may be lengthened and occur at less frequent intervals.

How Can Dynamically Oriented Art Therapy Reduce the Time Needed for Psychotherapeutic Treatment?

A number of psychiatrists and analysts have seen that the techniques of art therapy help to release deeply buried material more easily and thereby reduce the length of treatment, as well as mitigate the complications of the negative transference. It is observed that as his art expression improves, a patient becomes aware that by his understanding of the meaning of his own symbolic art, he is able to help actively in his own psychotherapy. His ego is thereby strengthened and his dependence on the therapist is gradually reduced.

How Important Is Transference in Dynamically Oriented Art Therapy?

In the beginning of this Introduction, reference was made to the indebtedness of dynamically oriented art therapy to Freud for an understanding of the various mechanisms of unconscious response and, especially, recognition of the importance of the role of transference and countertransference as it occurs in art therapy. In dynamically oriented art therapy, however, the transference of a patient is not only expressed verbally but is also projected visually in many pictures. But the transference relation in art therapy is considerably modified by the introduction of spontaneous images, for with the projection of images the patient, by means of free association, begins to understand more clearly the original objectification of his conflicts, which may have begun in his earliest family relationships. (Many aspects of the transference relation are expressed in the pictures of the first patient in this book.)

Has Dynamically Oriented Art Therapy Any Diagnostic Value?

The release of spontaneous images from the unconscious is regarded in art therapy as primarily a form of symbolic speech, but such images frequently have a diagnostic, as well as a therapeutic, value. Some spontaneous pictures created by patients show imaged patterns of response that are typical of specific mental illnesses. Schizophrenic thinking is, for instance, frequently expressed in the fragmented forms of certain pictures. A schizophrenic design, when explained by a patient, often uses a single image to represent an elaborate sequence of ideas.

An example of typical schizophrenic thinking was evident when a 17-year-old schizophrenic girl drew a picture of a pair of glasses posed on the large nose of her grandmother. Within both lenses of these glasses were drawn symbolic pictures. On the left lens she made some golden leaves. These, the patient said, represented the golden wedding of her grandparents. In the right lens she had drawn a complicated picture, comprehensible only with the help of the patient's explanation. The central dark oblong form, she said, was the grandfather's coffin. Her grandfather, she added, died soon after the golden wedding. The grandmother's heart with tears falling from it expressed the grandmother's grief at the loss of her husband. This drawing, using partial images to express a complicated symbolic meaning, is quite typical of schizophrenic thought and expresses the patient's own interpretation. No one but a schizophrenic could have drawn such a picture and offered such a complicated interpretation of its symbolic meaning.

Clearly diagnostic elements are frequently evident in the rigid geometric patterns of paranoid images. There is usually much black in the pictures of severely depressed patients. As an example, the depressed woman (the third case in this book) dramatized her depressed states in a number of pictures, sometimes dressing herself in black but frequently encasing her entire form in a black surround. (Other examples of diagnostic significance are evident in the spontaneous drawings of the two other case studies in this book.)

In the case study of the ulcer patient (the first in this book), the typical psychological responses to this condition are expressed in many of the pictures. Ulcer patients are frequently gifted and intelligent individuals who remain unaware of the degree of their unconscious dependency. This diagnostic element of the ulcer pattern is manifest in a number of the unconscious art projections of this patient, a female artist. Her unconscious wish to regress to infantile dependence is shown frequently in her pictures. These include a transference image in which the patient, as an infant, nurses at the therapist-mother's breast. A number of other drawings by this patient are expressions of a desire to return to the womb.

Another diagnostic element frequently found in the spontaneous images created by patients during art therapy is symbolic expression of either regression or progression in the therapeutic process. Changes in a series of symbolic images frequently inform the art therapist of positive changes in the course of a patient's treatment.

The diagnostic value of images created spontaneously by patients during dynamically oriented art therapy is of an entirely different order than those created in drawing tests given to patients by psychologists. The basic difference between these two approaches is that in art therapy the pictures created by patients are the patients' own *spontaneous*, unconscious projections, while the drawings created by patients under drawing test conditions are always prompted and are therefore planned for the purpose of obtaining a particular type of response to a given test. Although dynamically oriented art therapy and psychological drawing tests both use spontaneous drawings as a means of gaining insight into the unconscious emotional responses of patients, there is a fundamental difference in their purpose. In dynamically oriented art therapy the spontaneous images released by patients from their unconscious are in no way controlled by the therapist, but in drawing tests the form of each test demands specific types of responses within particular, defined limits.

Since the purpose and motivation of these two approaches differ fundamentally, it is important to point out that unconscious images released in dynamically oriented art therapy speak a symbolic language more closely allied to the free association method of classical psychoanalysis than the prompted method of drawing tests.

Can Dynamically Oriented Art Therapy Be Used in Groups?

The use of spontaneous art as an adjunct to other forms of psychotherapy in institutions dealing with disturbed children and adults is expanding. Some outstanding examples of such therapeutic and research projects are now in progress in a number of psychiatric hospitals, clinics and special schools. In most of these institutions psychotherapy is either psychoanalytically oriented or strongly influenced by the analytic approach. Consequently, whatever methods are employed by art therapists are adjusted to the specific psychiatric policies of these institutions. The focus of each art therapist is also quite naturally influenced by his professional background, training and special abilities.

Two aspects of what is in some hospitals considered as an "art" approach to patients—the teaching of art to psychiatric patients and the occupational therapy approach—do not qualify for the discussion here. These frequently encourage tracing, copying and dependence on molds, and are not the means of releasing spontaneous images from the unconscious. In the projects to be described, the art therapists mentioned are being accepted increasingly as part of the therapeutic team; they attend conferences and contribute reports that relate spontaneous art productions of patients to either diagnosis or therapy, or both.

In the application of art therapy to the treatment of groups, several significant new approaches have been developed that are of interest to further expansion of spontaneous art of psychotherapy. Two gifted women who have had professional training as artists, as well as experience in personal psychotherapy, have developed some interesting new techniques in dynamically oriented art therapy as applied to groups. Both have been able to develop their new approaches as staff members of psychiatric teams in two rather different psychiatric treatment and research centers.

The two women are Hanna Yaxa Kwiatkowska, a professional sculptor who is art therapist on the research project of the Section of Family Studies at the National Institute of Mental Health, Bethesda, Maryland, and Lynne Flexner Berger, a professional artist who directs the group-centered art therapy program at the Hospital of the Albert Einstein College of Medicine, New York City. Both women trained with the writer before undertaking their approaches to research in art therapy. In the psychiatric institutions where they developed their new group therapy approaches with spontaneous art, they had the active support of the psychiatrists and psychoanalysts.

Mrs. Kwiatkowska is the art therapist developing the art research project under Dr. Lyman Wynne, Director of the Adult Psychiatry Branch of the National Institute of Mental Health. Here art therapy is employed with individuals and family groups as a regular part of the program. The entire research project of which the art therapy is a part is described by Wynne as an investigation of "the psychodynamic interpretation of schizophrenia." In this program the techniques of art therapy are amplified to include the entire family group of the schizophrenic patient being studied. It is thus a supplementary research approach to the psychiatric treatment of family groups.

As Wynne has reported, art therapy is employed in this research program with both individuals and family groups:

> "Since 1953 the Section of Family Studies at the National Institute of Mental Health has been working on studies on developing a psychodynamic interpretation of schizophrenia that takes into account the social organization of the family as a whole. . . . Art therapy was introduced in 1958 as part of the general program and used with patients individually. Gradually the family was included in the art program.
>
> "We have also been gathering experience in the use of family sessions in which the family works conjointly in art therapy. We have examined the forms of perception and thinking manifest in the art productions of the family members both when they work on separate paintings and when they join together on the same painting. Both the art productions themselves and the family's interaction about them have contributed to our diagnostic evaluations and treatment program."[3]

Wynne also describes how sessions are tape-recorded and used in weekly conferences held between members of the therapeutic team.

Mrs. Kwiatkowska, as the art therapist on this research project, has indicated how, following art therapy sessions with individual schizophrenics selected originally for treatment, art therapy developed unexpectedly with the entire family of each of these patients:

> "It happened in several instances members of the family of the patient were on the ward at the time of the patient's individual art therapy session and asked to see the patient's productions—or the patient wished to have them at the session under one condition—that they would join the patient in his work. This proved to be an illuminating experience. The degree of involvement of other members of the family, the interaction with the patient, their joint discussion of the pictures was so revealing that this gave the incentive to include the family in the art therapy program."[4]

The art therapy program conducted by Lynne Flexner Berger with groups at the Day Hospital of the Albert Einstein College of Medicine, New York City, is known as Group-centered Art Therapy. This day hospital is a short-term treatment center of which Dr. Jack Wilder is the Director. Under the direction of Mrs. Berger, an interesting new approach to group art therapy has been

---

[3] Naumburg, Margaret: "Spontaneous Art in Psychotherapy." *Progress in Clinical Psychology* (Eds. L. E. Abt and B. F. Riess). New York, Grune and Stratton, 1963, Vol. V, pp. 83-84.
[4] *Ibid.*

developed. Small groups of patients take part in this project. Each week such a group is asked by Mrs. Berger to suggest and discuss what they would like to draw together on the large sheet of brown paper mounted on the wall. (The paper is about 36 by 60 inches in size.) The patients are offered pastels for this purpose. As the group art therapist has explained, "The patients frequently need help from me in order to work through their initial resistance to participation in the creation of a joint picture.

"When the group has decided on the subject for their panel, they all begin to draw on different sections of the sheet of paper. Sometimes the group agrees on a subject, but at other times each member of the group carries out his own ideas. When the group has selected a joint project, individuals may, nonetheless, draw something unrelated to the group decision."

Mrs. Berger not only encourages each group of patients to work out their own ideas for a panel, but she also remains as passive and nonjudgmental as possible in relation to their efforts. She is also prepared, when necessary, to alleviate anxiety or insecurity as expressed by individual patients or by group responses which might tend to block the creation of such a shared panel.

When a group feels that their panel is finished (which usually takes about 30 to 45 minutes), they then discuss their picture with Mrs. Berger and they are encouraged to express their free associations to their art production. The individual members of each group are also encouraged by the art therapist to express their personal problems and conflicts in the presence of the other patients so that these matters can be shared and reacted to by the entire group.

The interaction of patients in these group discussions has proved of diagnostic value as well as of therapeutic benefit to individual patients. Frequently the art therapist's diagnosis of individual patients in these groups is the same as that made by the clinician who has analyzed the individual responses of the same patients.

A Third Approach to Group Art Therapy

There is yet another approach to group art therapy in which spontaneous art can be employed as a supplement to the generally accepted techniques used in verbal group therapy. In a study on "The Use of Spontaneous Art in Dynamically Oriented Group Therapy of Obese Women" by the writer in collaboration with Dr. Janet Caldwell, spontaneous art productions were encouraged among a group of obese women who were included in a group research project at the Bureau of Nutrition, Department of Health, City of New York. These obese women had failed to reduce on the obesity diet prescribed by this clinic. They were then organized in an experimental group to use spontaneous art as an addition to verbal group therapy.[5]

This experimental research, adapting spontaneous art expression into verbal group therapy with obese women, was not for the purpose of reducing the obese

[5] Naumburg, Margaret, and Caldwell, Janet: "The Use of Spontaneous Art in Dynamically Oriented Group Therapy of Obese Women." Paper presented at the Second Internation Congress of Psychiatry, Zurich, September, 1957. *Acta Psychother.* (Basel) 7:254-287, 1959.

women, but with the intention of investigating their significant emotional attitudes and psychological responses. The results of 18 months of combined group and art therapy provided the evidence, through spontaneous art productions, that the personality patterns of these seven obese women were similar. The psychological value of art as a means of exploring the dynamics of obesity had not, according to available reports, been previously explored. Many of the typical responses of patients in the literature on obesity were confirmed in the art productions of this group of women.

These women presented a rather consistent personality pattern, classified within the personality trait disturbance of passive-aggressive personality, and as belonging to the subgroup, passive dependent.[6] Their spontaneous art productions illustrated many aspects of the recognized personality pattern of obese women. These rather isolated women were able to communicate more freely through their typical art productions, which related directly to their problems of obesity and led to the consequent freeing of their verbal communication with each other and with the co-therapists. This helped to release much repressed material which had not previously been verbalized and in consequence speeded up the therapeutic process.

The work with obese women was only an initial experimental research effort in introducing, into group therapy, spontaneous art in combination with verbalization. Much more research is needed into how spontaneous art productions of various types of mental patients could be aided with the addition of spontaneous art to the verbal aspects of group therapy now in use both in hospitals and in private practice.

How Is Dynamically Oriented Art Therapy Different from Occupational Therapy?

Occupational therapy is frequently confused with art therapy by the uninitiated because occupational therapy employs methods of developing arts and crafts in the activities of hospitalized patients. Occupational therapy is employed to a great extent with patients who have physical disabilities and is applicable only to a limited degree with psychiatric patients. This is because of the way occupational therapy developed as a method of rehabilitation during the First World War. Much of the training of occupational therapists deals with the problems of physical rehabilitation. When art materials are employed by occupational therapists with patients, such activity is usually considered a form of occupation to fill the long and empty hours of hospitalization. Original art expression is not therefore the primary goal of the teaching of arts and crafts by occupational therapists. Their emphasis tends to be placed on the copying and tracing of patterns and also on the use of formal molds rather than on the encouragement of original expression in art. Those trained in occupational therapy have not, in the past, emphasized sufficiently the importance of the unconscious responses of hospitalized patients through the development of spontaneous art expression, but lately a growing number of occupational therapists have

---

[6] *Diagnostic & Statistical Manual, Mental Disorders.* Washington, D.C., American Psychiatric Association, 1952.

become interested in gaining an understanding of dynamically oriented art therapy. Such occupational therapists, after receiving practical orientation in the development of spontaneous art productions with their patients, are now beginning to use art therapy in cooperation with psychiatrists at a number of state and city hospitals. Such a change in the training of occupational therapists has been encouraged by Professor Frieda Behlen, Director of Occupational Therapy at New York University, who has urged her students to learn how to employ art therapy as a part of their training.

Art therapy, in contrast to occupational therapy, is dynamically oriented and its treatment depends on the transference relation between patient and therapist. It therefore encourages the spontaneous creation of pictures or sculpture as a means of releasing unconscious conflicts, phantasies and dreams with the help of the analytic technique of free association.

Who Can Work with Dynamically Oriented Art Therapy?

It is natural to have this question asked in relation to the new psychotherapeutic technique of art therapy. It is often assumed mistakenly that only those with previous art training can work with art therapy. Previous art training can be an asset, but unless such special training includes a background in abnormal psychology and, when possible, some personal psychotherapy, students cannot be adequately trained to become art therapists.

Psychiatric interns who show interest in art therapy frequently ask whether any art background is essential. It is the experience of this writer that a well-trained psychotherapist who has a sympathetic interest in any of the creative arts is able to encourage effectively his patient's creative efforts. Only a psychotherapist who lacks interest in any of the arts would be unable to use dynamically oriented art therapy with his patients. What is essential, then, to a psychotherapist who wishes to learn how to use the art therapy approach is not that he be able to create pictures himself, but that he have a sympathy for and understanding of the creative efforts of his patients and that he believe in their creative potentiality. He may already have an interest in the arts—such as music, drama or dance—which would be helpful in dealing with the artistic efforts of his patients, but for those therapists who have no interest in any of the arts, the techniques of art therapy could never become useful.

How Does Dynamically Oriented Art Therapy Differ from Art Teaching?

As already explained, dynamically oriented art therapy is a form of psychotherapy which does not teach but, by various techniques already described, has as its objective the recovery or readjustment of a patient to himself and to his environment. Spontaneous art expression, while important, is but one element of the therapeutic methods employed in art therapy. The art productions of a patient undergoing treatment by means of art therapy are released, it must be remembered, through the unconscious projection of images, produced within the transference relation.

Art teaching, in contrast to art therapy, is a conscious teaching method which seeks to improve or expand a pupil's skill in various forms of art expression. It employs conscious methods and techniques of art expression. Therefore, although dynamically oriented art therapy and art teaching both make use of art, their goals are entirely different. Art therapy encourages the release of spontaneous imagery from the unconscious of patients; art teaching is a planned and conscious process for improving the art productions of students.

What Art Materials Are Needed for Art Therapy?

For those patients who have never drawn or painted before undertaking art therapy (this includes the majority of patients), it is necessary to have simple art media which can be easily and quickly manipulated. During the early therapy sessions, time must be spent with these patients in demonstrating and explaining usable techniques for helping to free unconscious dreams, phantasies and repressed emotions into imaged expression. Experience has shown that certain art materials are the most suitable for releasing spontaneous art expressions easily and quickly. That is the reason that semihard pastels and casein, or poster paints, are preferred. (Oil paints are not generally used with beginners because they take too long to dry and are more difficult to handle.)

Practice in the use of the art media must be carefully explained to patients inexperienced in painting or drawing, so as to help them release their unconscious imaged projections. After a preliminary explanation to patients as to the several ways in which pastels can be employed to express changing moods and phantasies, they are given a practical demonstration of how to apply what is known as the "scribble" technique.

While the patient who has never drawn or painted before may be shy and hesitant in his first attempts at pictorial expression, the professional artist who comes to art therapy for the first time has a very different problem. Since he has professional training in the use of color and form, he usually tends to be self-conscious at the beginning of therapy and unable to forget all that he knows about creative art. But an artist's greatest anxiety in undertaking art therapy is that the art therapist may interfere with the originality of his creative expression, in spite of the fact that a professional artist usually seeks art therapy because his creative expression is blocked or not functioning.

The "Scribble" Technique as Applied in Art Therapy

The "scribble" technique is demonstrated to the patients in art therapy as a means of helping to liberate their spontaneous expression. It requires the use of large sheets of paper and either pastels or poster paints. Each patient is helped to relax body tension in order to do his drawing freely. The patients are encouraged to draw without conscious planning by making a continuous and unpremeditated flowing line while keeping pastel or paint brush always on paper. Such a spontaneous line may cross and recross the paper many times in irregular patterning. The patient is then asked to look at his scribble pattern and try to discover some suggestion of a design, or possibly an object, person, animal or landscape. If nothing is suggested to him in the original position of the paper, it can be turned to the other three sides and the elements of a suggestive image can then be elaborated or modified. This drawing is not prompted as in the Rorschach or other drawing tests, for in scribble drawing the original pattern is created by the patient and he is encouraged to develop any image that his scribble lines suggest. The purpose of such spontaneous drawing is therefore not primarily diagnostic, as in drawing tests, but is intended to release spontaneous images from the unconscious of the patient or pupil. The pictures are then of value in art therapy as a means of encouraging free associations. (The three cases described later illustrate the application of the scribble technique.)

III. HOW DYNAMICALLY ORIENTED ART THERAPY DIFFERS FROM OTHER PSYCHOTHERAPEUTIC APPROACHES

Differences between Views of Dynamically Oriented Art Therapy and Freudian Psychoanalysis

The art therapist, like the psychoanalyst, encourages the patient to develop free associations to his pictures, whether they express dreams, phantasies, wishes, etc., in exactly the same way as a Freudian analyst obtains free associations to a patient's dreams. An art therapist, however, cannot remain as passive as a Freudian analyst, for the role of an art therapist is comparable to that of such psychoanalysts as Sullivan, Horney, Fromm and others who place emphasis on the active interpersonal relation between analyst and analysand.

When Dr. René Spitz, one of the outstanding older Freudian analysts, spoke as the chief discussant in a symposium on art therapy at an annual meeting of the American Orthopsychiatric Association,[7] he began his discussion by first introducing his own experience in using art therapy with certain patients whom he described as having "great difficulty in speaking, who are severely depressed, apathetic and negative." He described the particular method that he had employed in order to obtain the desired pictures. He engaged an art teacher in order to get these patients to paint pictures in her presence. She was expected to offer such patients the needed art supplies, but she was asked by Dr. Spitz to make no comment nor to ask the patients anything about their pictures. These art productions were then brought to Dr. Spitz by the patients at their next analytic sessions.

According to Spitz, he was then able, with the help of the pictures produced under the limited conditions that he had devised, to get some particularly difficult patients to speak more freely about themselves and their problems. It was in this way that he found that the introduction of art therapy into the analysis of borderline and depressed patients could be helpful in analytic treatment.

Spitz stated what he thought were the fundamental differences between classical psychoanalysis and art therapy:

---

[7] September, 1954, New York City. Quoted from Spitz' unpublished manuscript, by permission.

"While in analytical therapy the analyst remains anonymous, non-interfering, does not manipulate the patient and stays extremely passive, the situation in art therapy by its very nature is completely different. Art therapy, of necessity, takes place in a social situation. The therapist has to manipulate the patient to a certain extent; the therapist has to interfere to a certain extent and can by no means remain as passive and certainly not as anonymous as the analyst."[8]

Such a statement shows a misunderstanding of the way in which treatment by means of art therapy differs from Freudian analysis. Certainly the patient reclining on a couch and speaking to an invisible analyst could not create spontaneous art under these conditions. When Spitz stated that art therapy takes place in a social situation and that the art therapist has to manipulate the patient, he has misunderstood the process, for he has assumed that all spontaneous art productions are, in art therapy, produced in the presence of the art therapist. This, however, does not always happen. Many of the spontaneous pictures made by patients are created either at home or on the hospital ward between art therapy sessions. They are then shown to the therapist in the following therapy session. (How such pictures are used to obtain "free associations" by patients in art therapy can be clearly understood by following the three cases of emotionally disturbed women in this book.)

The art therapist introduces patients to certain techniques that will help free them—rather than, as Dr. Spitz implies, "manipulate the patient"—in the spontaneous expression of their thoughts, feelings and memories. These techniques include ways of relaxing muscles, freeing spontaneous body movements and demonstrations of the "scribble" technique.

The activity of a patient in dynamically oriented art therapy does not only consist of expression through spontaneous pictures, but also includes much verbal communication with the art therapist, centering around the patient's conflicts and problems, that may or may not have already been expressed in his pictures. How each patient may choose to employ spontaneous art expression depends on each patient's individual needs whether he uses it constantly or intermittently, or only during critical phases of therapy. When art therapy and its techniques are introduced to a patient depends on the type of patient and his particular needs; the use of these techniques may vary considerably, as many sessions may be partially or entirely verbal, whenever either patient or therapist finds this more appropriate.

Spitz also examined the difference between transference as understood in classical analysis and transference as employed in art therapy. He made a distinction between the two approaches which tends to offer a superficial and mistaken interpretation of the role of transference in art therapy. He described transference in psychoanalysis as "in the nature of something secret going on between him (the patient) and the therapist," and then suggested: "It is quite

---

[8] Naumburg, Margaret: "Spontaneous Art in Psychotherapy." *Op. cit.,* pp. 75-76.

different in art therapy. The product in art therapy is something that is socially accepted; it is approved of; it may be praised; it represents a valuable narcissistic gratification."[9]

Spitz further discussed when and how art expression may be valuable and remarked that in his experience with the analysis of artists, their art had revealed little significant data concerning themselves. This, he explained, was due to the fact that artist patients have learned to conceal their emotional problems in their work. However, if his artist patients had been introduced to the techniques of dynamically oriented art therapy, they might well have revealed as much of their repressed conflicts as did the professional artist patient described in this book.

Although Spitz's experiments with art therapy were limited to a small number of nonverbal patients drawing their pictures in the presence of an art teacher who was asked not to communicate with them about their art work, other Freudian analysts will be mentioned later who have found it possible to encourage their patients to bring their original art productions to the analytic sessions.

The unconscious meanings of the spontaneous art productions created during art therapy are frequently obtained by encouraging the patient's free associations to the images he creates. Such pictures are often a direct form of communication that functions as symbolic speech. It is sometimes difficult to convey to psychoanalysts accustomed only to communication through words that a primary nonverbal technique such as art therapy can effectively release many repressed feelings of a patient more directly and more swiftly than words. Furthermore, a patient who projects his conflicts and the stages of ego development into images frequently becomes able to interpret their symbolic meaning correctly himself, without assistance from the art therapist.

Anyone who has read the writer's publications dealing with illustrated cases of patients treated by means of analytically oriented art therapy will recognize that the majority of images created are intimate and confidential revelations of unconscious conflicts expressed in symbolic form; they rarely achieve the status which Spitz referred to as "socially accepted art." However, by means of dynamically oriented art therapy, some patients have been helped to recover their previously blocked creative abilities.

An interesting point concerning the nature of spontaneous art productions in psychotherapy was suggested by Spitz when he referred to the kinesthetic perceptions which become reactivated or acted out in action painting. This, he suggested, confronts us with an exciting proposition because art therapy thus becomes a way of expression and of communication on a different psychic level. "Then, the paintings have a function as a facilitator, an accelerator of communication, and one might well speculate on the possibility of art activity being part of a therapeutic process which would facilitate the 'insight' through the reliving of an experience in the form of an action."[10] To state this concept in terms of

---

[9] *Ibid.*, p. 76.
[10] *Ibid.*

dynamically oriented art therapy, the making of spontaneous images helps to speed up the process of therapy because it deals with a deep and universal symbolic language of man derived from the unverbalized depths of the unconscious.

When a few Freudian analysts accepted the spontaneous art productions of their patients, such pictures were usually interpreted by them in the same way as they would interpret the symbolism of dreams or phantasies, without encouraging their patients' free associations to the meaning of their pictures. The writer has previously discussed the limitations of the traditional analytic approach to the spontaneous art of patients in reference to a report by the psychoanalyst Dr. Gustav Bychowski, which interprets his patients' pictures from the limited viewpoint of the classical analytic approach.[11]

Another Freudian, Dr. Max M. Stern, has shown a greater appreciation of the value of spontaneous art in relation to psychoanalysis than did Bychowski.[12] Stern uses his patients' "free paintings" primarily in relation to childhood memories. Stern also interprets the art expression of his patients himself, in analytic terms, primarily in relation to "the oral and oedipal drama," but more than any Freudian he has recognized the value of obtaining from his patients "free" associations to such symbolic pictures. Whatever images Stern's patients produce are, however, always interpreted by him in strictly Freudian terms. Stern however, encouraged "free painting" by his patients, and he has described how free association to such pictures can be useful in a Freudian analysis:

> "The effect of this method [free painting] is to enrich and activate the analysis. The intensification achieved by the introduction of this method into an analysis that is already under way is often surprising to the analyst and to the patient, both as regards the production of material and the changes resulting from integration of the material. It seems that the effect emanating from a picture reaches into the unconscious more deeply than does that of language due to the fact that pictorial expression is more adequate to the developmental state in which the training occurred; it has remained more within the range of the concrete and physical than has the verbal expression."[13]

This statement is important since it shows that a Freudian analyst has discovered, through his own particular methods of treatment, the great value of imaged expression within a classical analysis. However, it also illustrates the extent to which Freudians emphasize the primary influence of the early oedipal phase, but do not relate the encouragement of spontaneous art expression as an aid to the final integration of their patients.

---

[11] Bychowski, G.: "The Rebirth of a Woman: a Psychoanalytic Study of Artistic Expression and Sublimation." *Psychoanal. Rev.* 34:32-57, 1947. Discussed by Naumburg, Margaret: *Schizophrenic Art: Its Meaning in Psychotherapy.* New York, Grune & Stratton, 1950, pp. 26-32.

[12] Stern, M. M. "Free Painting as an Auxiliary Technique in Psychoanalysis." *Specialized Techniques in Psychotherapy* (Eds. G. Bychowski and J. Louise Despert). New York, Basic Books, 1952, pp. 65-83.

[13] *Ibid.,* p. 80.

Although Stern recognizes the value of "free painting," few of his Freudian colleagues have been ready to encourage their patients to express themselves in this way. Stern, however, refers to the fact that psychoanalysis has long accepted the method of free expression in the form of pictures as a representation of unconscious processes.

While maintaining the orthodox Freudian treatment with the patient on the couch during analytic sessions, Stern encouraged patients to make free paintings at home and bring them to the sessions. His approach is limited by the fact that he regards the free associations obtained from these paintings as primarily reinforcing "the role of the oedipal triad—the primal scene, infantile masturbation and pavor nocturnus."[14]

Stern describes how he encourages his patients to create free paintings at home:

> "When the analysis is under way, the patient is informed that the treatment may be intensified by his painting pictures at home. . . . He is to exclude all conscious direction as much as possible, and thus to produce a picture which corresponds to a free idea (freier Einfall). . . . The patient is asked to abstain from any evaluation or criticism while he paints . . . whether or not the drawing meets his expectations and whether or not he finds it pleasing."[15]

In Stern's approach to the use of art therapy the patient's freedom to associate to his spontaneous art productions is severely limited by the orders of the analyst, for the patient is told to exclude all conscious expectations; therefore there is no chance for the patient to freely interpret the meaning of his pictures to the therapist. In contrast to this formal Freudian use of a patient's art productions to reinforce his analytic approach, dynamically oriented art therapy allows a patient complete freedom to associate to his symbolic art productions in any way that he chooses.

Dr. Stern has stated:

> "Like dreams, the paintings thus produced are determined by unconscious processes; they, too, reveal their latent meaning only through free associations. . . . The patients' associations to the pictures lead, in almost all cases, first, to the memory of the recent experience which occasioned the painting; second, to an abundance of childhood memories. . . . These childhood memories are screen memories for typical earlier traumatic events, especially of the oral and oedipal phases."[16]

Stern has developed a technique for obtaining spontaneous art projections from the unconscious of his patients. Its function is carefully limited to the Freudian approach and emphasizes a patient's art primarily in relation to early traumatic experiences. The symbolic projections of Stern's patients show in their spontaneity a certain similarity to images produced in the art expression

---

[14] *Ibid.*, p. 68.
[15] *Ibid.*, p. 66.
[16] *Ibid.*, p. 67.

of some patients treated by means of dynamically oriented art therapy. For instance, one of Stern's patients used red and black symbolically to represent hate of the father. Such use of red and black combined to express hate of a parent of either sex occurs frequently in the writer's experience in the use of dynamically oriented art therapy.

In reference to one of his patients, Stern describes his image of a spider as a symbol of the mother. This symbol has also been used by one of the writer's patients in art therapy to represent the mother. Stern encourages "free association" to their paintings by his patients in a way that is similar to the method used in dynamically oriented art therapy, but he controls the conditions within which the patients are expected to reveal the meaning of their art productions. If more freedom were permitted to his analytic patients, they might have released more significant material beyond traumatic experiences of childhood, which are of so much concern to the Freudian analysts.

In dynamically oriented art therapy, a broader range of free associations is encouraged than seems evident in psychoanalytic procedures, and consequently much significant data—which patients were afraid, as yet, to verbalize—is frequently released through dynamically oriented art therapy.

Rollo May, in his paper "Creativity and Encounter," has discussed a negative attitude toward creativity among psychoanalysts. He quotes Ernest Kris' well-known formulation of art expression as "regression in the service of ego" and analyzes this generally accepted analytic interpretation of creativity as being limited by its negative element in the process of creation.

While admitting the existence of regressive elements, in symbol and myth, as emphasized by psychoanalysts, May expands his own interpretation of these aspects of the creative process:

> "Symbol and myth do bring into awareness the infantile, archaic, unconscious longings, dreads and similar psychic content. . . . this is their regressive aspect. But they also bring out new meaning, new forms, disclose reality, which was literally not present before, a reality that is not merely subjective but has one pole which is outside ourselves. . . . this is the *progressive* side of symbol and myth. This aspect points ahead—is integrative. . . . *It is this second, progressive aspect of symbols and myths that is almost completely omitted in the traditional Freudian psychoanalytic approach.*"[17] [Italics this writer's.]

May's emphasis on the progressive as well as the regressive aspects in psychotherapy is one which is clearly demonstrated in the cases of the treatment of three disturbed women in this book.

Differences and Similarities between Dynamic Art Therapy and Jungian Analytic Psychology

Jung also questioned the reductive and negative aspect of Freud's approach and chose a broader interpretation of the unconscious as being both collective and personal. Although Freud did not respond to the wish of some of his patients

---

[17] May, R.: "Creativity and Encounter." *Amer. J. Psychoanal.* 24 (No. 1):42, 1964.

to draw their dreams, Jung frequently encouraged the expression of dreams and phantasies in pictures by his patients. He had discovered through his patients' comments the positive value of expressive painting as a more direct means than words for dealing with unconscious nonverbal experiences in psychotherapy.

When one of Jung's patients had a vivid dream and told him, "Do you know, if only I were a painter I would make a picture of it,"[18] Jung would urge him to try to draw or paint it. From his many experiences with both professional artists and those who had never drawn before, Jung remarked, "To paint what we see before us is a different art from painting what we see within."[19]

Regardless of the fact that Freud rejected and Jung accepted the use of symbolic art expression in psychotherapy, dynamically oriented art therapy cannot be tied to any one specific scientific interpretation of the significance of spontaneous art or dream productions. Dynamically oriented art therapy leaves a patient free to direct his associations to the images he creates in any direction that he chooses. It therefore frees the patient from overdependence on the art therapist and also speeds up the therapeutic procedure.

How the American Approach to Art Therapy Differs from the European Approach to Psychopathologic Art

There are several reasons for the difference in orientation between the European and American approach to the art of mental patients—reasons which relate to the difference in the background of the European psychiatrists who have turned to the study of the esthetic quality of the art productions of schizophrenic patients in the large psychiatric hospitals of Europe. The original interest of these European psychiatrists was stirred by the publication in 1922 of Prinzhorn's book, *Bildnerei der Geisteskranken*. The book was based on collected paintings, drawings and sculpture of a group of schizophrenic patients in Europe. Through the publication of Prinzhorn's book, not only European psychiatrists but also a wider public became acquainted for the first time with the remarkable quality of schizophrenic art. As I wrote about 15 years ago:

"Prinzhorn's book stands as a landmark in the study of psychotic art. Its many color reproductions are magnificent and its text offers the most complete survey of the literature on the subject up to that time. While its practical use as a reference book remains unchallenged, the inadequacy of Prinzhorn's text seems to have received too little criticism.

"The reproductions in Prinzhorn's book were drawn from a vast collection of psychotic art known as the Heidelberg collection, which he had gathered from many of the insane asylums of Europe. As in the earlier collections of psychotic art, the data on the clinical histories of patients were second hand and often inaccurate. The art products had been selected first and supplementary information concerning long institutionalized patients had then been collected. . . .

---

[18] Jung, Carl: "The Aims of Psychotherapy." *The Practice of Psychotherapy*, Bollingen Series XX. New York, Pantheon, 1954, Chap. IV, p. 47.
[19] *Ibid.*, p. 50.

"Prinzhorn expressed himself as critical of the known approaches to psychotic art, which he referred to as 'the psychiatric,' 'the folklore' and the 'psychoanalytic' approach; his own viewpoint, based on gestalt psychology, defended what he called the 'esthetic' approach. His attempts to define the esthetic value of psychotic art were based on vague generalizations such as, "Pictures made by human hands reach up into their own sphere of values which can only be directly experienced as esthetic!"[20]

In the United States the methods of psychoanalysis and its understanding of the unconscious responses of various types of mental patients has penetrated into all the psychiatric teaching of our medical schools, as well as into the training of residents in state and veterans hospitals. Practicing physicians, including pediatricians, absorbed much about unconscious motivations and its relation to all forms of illness. In many parts of Europe, however, it seems that even the indirect influence of psychoanalytic method is still rejected by the directors of the large psychiatric hospitals.

In the United States the difference between the psychiatric attitude toward the treatment of regressed or chronic schizophrenics and those who are not so severely ill is quite marked. It is true that like the large psychiatric hospitals in Europe, the state, city and veterans hospitals of the United States contain large numbers of regressed schizophrenics who seem unable to respond to any form of psychotherapy. Nevertheless, in some large psychiatric hospitals in the United States, there are patients who respond surprisingly well to forms of dynamically oriented psychotherapy.

The fact that American psychiatrists and psychoanalysts have been successful in various forms of psychotherapeutic treatment of the less severe forms of schizophrenia is a hopeful sign. Because of the belief in the possibility of using psychotherapy effectively with certain types of schizophrenics, the development of dynamically oriented art therapy procedures became possible.

There are two recent European publications that deserve consideration as an aid to our understanding of the European psychiatric attitude concerning the value of the art productions of schizophrenic patients. One is *Though This Be Madness: a Study in Psychotic Art*,[21] in which several well known European psychiatrists, who are directors of psychiatric hospitals, show that their attitudes toward the value of the art of schizophrenic patients are based on their special esthetic quality. Dr. Alfred Bader explained that the purpose of this volume, which offers some striking pictures done by regressed schizophrenics, is to intrigue laymen through its emphasis on an esthetic rather than a therapeutic approach to the art of schizophrenics. Bader, like the Dutch psychiatrist, Dr. J. H. Plokker, the director of a psychiatric hospital in the Netherlands, regards the pictures of schizophrenic patients as unfathomable. In referring to the pictures

---

[20] Naumburg, Margaret: *Schizophrenic Art: Its Meaning in Psychotherapy*. New York, Grune & Stratton, 1950, pp. 10-11.

[21] *Though This Be Madness: a Study in Psychotic Art*. Revised by Alfred Bader. Original Swiss edition, *Insania Pingens*, Ciba, Basel, 1961; also in English. London. Thames & Hudson, 1961.

of the three schizophrenic patients in this book, Bader writes: "Not only do they reveal in admirable fashion hidden, undiscovered talent, but they also furnish evidence of that eternal humanity which is ever present, even in the schizophrenic whose mental disease has placed him beyond the pale of society."[22] Dr. Hans Steck, another psychiatrist who comments in this book on the art of schizophrenics, writes: "In the delusions of schizophrenics we are confronted with thought patterns of such impenetrability that all attempts to attribute meaning to them in terms comprehensible to us have long since been abandoned."[23]

Dr. J. H. Plokker has expressed similar views in his book on the art productions of schizophrenics, *Artistic Self-Expression in Mental Disease*, which also deals entirely with schizophrenic art productions. He writes: "The schizophrenic knows no development in the positive sense; he retraces his own steps in regressive or, if it is desired to avoid this term, reverts of necessity to primitive forms of expression and design, because of the loss of his higher mental powers."[24]

These three statements from European psychiatrists who direct large psychiatric hospitals are quoted to show that although they refer to the writings of Freud and Jung, they are as yet unaware of the important role of the unconscious in psychotherapy.

The group of European psychiatrists who are united in the organization Societé Internationale de Psychopathologie de l'Expression are primarily concerned with the esthetic quality rather than the symbolic imagery of the art of schizophrenic patients; consequently, they are not concerned with any form of art therapy.

Plokker expressed what is typical of the traditional psychiatrists in this European organization. He explained his views on what he calls "creative" therapy in the following way:

"The typical character of the individual does not lie in the unconscious, the 'Id' (Es), but in the conscious, the 'ego' (Ich). It has repeatedly been pointed out—most recently and very positively by Rümke—that the problem in schizophrenia is not one of content but of *form*. There will therefore not be detailed descriptions of what the drawings really do represent. It is, in fact, not a question of *what* is represented, but *how* it is portrayed."[25]

The three case studies of three women in this book as well as many other case studies in dynamically oriented art therapy demonstrate that it is impossible to separate form from content. This is confirmed by the creative work of all outstanding artists.

Plokker warns in his book that it is dangerous to allow schizophrenic patients to indulge in free art expression because "If a schizophrenic patient

---

[22] *Ibid.*, pp. 33-34.
[23] *Ibid.*, p. 21.
[24] Plokker, J. H.: *Artistic Self-Expression in Mental Disease*. London, Mouton & Co., 1964, p. 73. Title of American edition changed to *Art from the Mentally Disturbed*. Boston, Little, Brown & Co., 1965.
[25] *Ibid.*, p. 6.

is allowed to work freely he will become even more submerged in his morbid thoughts and turn even more from reality, become more involved in his delusions and even more directed to his hallucinations."[26] In order, therefore, to overcome what he considers the dangers of autism, he directs the attention of his schizophrenic patients to the external world by encouraging them to draw still life objects, portraits, and actual landscapes.

Plokker has in his methods, as he admits, followed the accepted approach of occupational therapy. By controlling the art of schizophrenics in this formal way, he has bypassed the practical experiences of dynamically oriented art therapists who have employed effectively the free associations of schizophrenics and other mental patients as a means of uncovering unconscious conflicts. He also described the traditional approach of psychiatry to the mental patient. Occupational therapy, which he identified with his own interpretation of "creative therapy," has now in the United States (if not in Europe) been gradually influenced by the practice of dynamic psychiatry to become more aware of the role of the unconscious in the life of mental patients. As a consequence, some of the leaders in the education of occupational therapists are urging their students to obtain training in dynamically oriented art therapy.

Plokker imposes a superficial discipline upon his schizophrenic patients, but in a sound psychotherapeutic approach in dynamic art therapy the patient learns to understand the nature of his unconscious conflicts, so that he is himself able to develop a certain self-discipline toward his problems. A patient in such art therapy, because he begins to understand his problems through their spontaneous art projection, becomes able to begin to discipline and guide himself without the dominating control of a therapist.

Plokker spends considerable space in his book on downgrading the psychiatrists who in private practice deal with schizophrenics, for he assumes that if a schizophrenic patient is hospitalized on the advice of his psychiatrist, such a physician has no further contact with his patient and therefore remains ignorant of the later phases of his patient's mental illness. He states, "The psychiatrists and psychologists attached to a mental hospital are really the only persons who know the clinical picture in all its variety."[27] He further elaborates this viewpoint when he says, "Psychiatrists in normal city practice, assistants in a university clinic, who can seldom observe patients for more than a few months, have only a very limited knowledge of schizophrenia."[28]

Dynamically oriented art therapy is based on a recognition that when the unconscious conflicts of mental patients are released through their free associations to their spontaneous art, other procedures of psychotherapy can be successfully carried out. Without a full understanding of the mechanisms of dynamic psychiatry, the treatment of various types of mental patients by means of dynamically oriented art therapy is not possible.

---

[26] *Ibid.*, p. 120.
[27] *Ibid.*, p. 7.
[28] *Ibid.*, p. 12.

How Two Foreign Developments of Symbolic Techniques in Psychotherapy Supplement the Techniques of Dynamic Art Therapy

Two very different foreign approaches which emphasize new symbolic techniques have contributed some important additions to the treatment of schizophrenics.

"Symbolic Realization" as Developed by M. A. Sechehaye

In her important book *Symbolic Realization: A New Method of Psychotherapy*, M. A. Sechehaye, a Swiss psychoanalyst, has described her approach to the treatment of a severely ill schizophrenic girl when many forms of psychotherapy had failed.[29]

The second book, by an Australian psychiatrist, Dr. Ainslie Meares, is *The Door of Serenity, a Study in the Therapeutic Use of Symbolic Painting*.[30] This study, like that by Mme. Sechehaye, also describes the successful treatment of a seriously ill schizophrenic girl who had failed, previously, to respond to other forms of treatment.

In contrast to the books published by European psychiatrists belonging to the Societé Internationale de Psychopathologie de L'Expression, these two books by psychotherapists of different cultural backgrounds and training have both proved the effectiveness of their own particular methods through which both therapists encouraged the creation of spontaneous pictures or actions in the course of the treatment of two severely ill schizophrenic young patients. Meares obtained paintings from a schizophrenic young woman patient after insulin coma and electric shock treatment had been tried and failed. Sechehaye developed experimentally a new method of psychotherapy that she called "symbolic realization" when she found that psychoanalysis could not lead to the recovery of the schizophrenic girl she was treating. Although her patient made many symbolic drawings in the course of treatment which supplemented this new technique of active symbolic realization, what is of greatest importance to those concerned with dynamically oriented art therapy is that Sechehaye developed an effective new nonverbal method through the use of symbolic objects which satisfied the regressed condition of the schizophrenic girl.

Sechehaye explained: "Renée had not yet reached the stage of verbal language when the primary traumata occurred." In the case of Renée, a concrete nonverbal response was needed, she said, because Renée had a conflict which occurred prior to the formation of the ego.

When Sechehaye recognized that Renée was incapable of understanding her speech, she realized that only through symbolic images could she communicate with her young patient. The clue to the direct symbolic response with Renée occurred over the symbolism of apples which the girl related to the early deprivation of milk from her mother in infancy.

---

[29] Sechehaye, M. A.: *Symbolic Realization: A New Method of Psychotherapy*. New York, International Universities Press, 1951.

[30] Meares, A.: *The Door of Serenity, a study in the Therapeutic Use of Symbolic Painting*. Springfield, Ill., Charles C Thomas, 1958.

Sechehaye explained how this realization had come to her as she noted that "in order to express her need for receiving maternal food, Renée picks the green apples from the trees. (These green apples, still attached to the tree, stand for the mother.) The patient must pick them herself, since the mother does not give them to her."[31] Sechehaye offered the patient many beautiful apples but these were rejected by the girl.

"I persist in trying to understand the symbolism of the apples. To the remark that I gave her as many apples as she wanted, Renée cries, 'Yes, but those are store apples, apples for big people, but I want apples from Mummy, like that,' pointing to my breasts. 'Those apples there, Mummy gives them only when one is hungry.'

"I understand at last what must be done. Since apples represent maternal milk, I must give them to her like a mother feeding her baby. I must give her the symbol myself, directly and without intermediary— and at a fixed hour. To verify my hypothesis I carry it out at once. Taking an apple, and cutting it in two, I offer Renée a piece, saying, 'It is time to drink the good milk from Mummy's apples. Mummy is going to give it to you.' Renée then leans up against my shoulder, presses the apple upon my breast, and very solemnly, with intense happiness, eats it.

"The symbolism of the apples was . . . revival of all the shocks that Renée had had in infancy in regard to food, which represents maternal love.

"However, in order to make herself understood and solve the conflict, the 'loving mother' also had to find something other than the verbal method of psychoanalysis, because the initial conflict occurred before the development of spoken language and because the patient had regressed to the stage of magic presymbolic participation. The mode had to be more primitive and had to correspond to the stage at which the training had taken place. The only one that could be used was that which is suitable to the baby; expression by the symbolic signs of gestures and movements."[32]

"Symbolic Painting" as Used by Dr. Ainslie Meares

The second severely ill schizophrenic girl was treated by Meares with what he called "the use of a symbolic painting," only after she had been treated unsuccessfully with insulin coma and electric shock, and by narcoanalysis. After many months of such treatment, she was "so inhibited and withdrawn," writes Meares, "that it was practically impossible to get her to talk."

When this young girl, Jennifer, offered Meares a painting at one of her almost inarticulate sessions, he began to ask her about the meaning of this strange symbolic design and the many others that she would continue to bring to the sessions. Their patterns were strangely bizarre and difficult to decipher, even with the patient's brief comments, but he gradually accumulated her comments about these paintings and discovered specific meanings and associations to certain of her symbols.

---

[31] Sechehaye, M. A.: *Op. cit.*, p. 68.
[32] *Ibid.*, pp. 50-51.

In his nontechnical description of the unconscious motivation of this schizo-phrenic girl's spontaneous art productions, Meares carefully avoids the use of any psychoanalytic terminology concerning the mechanisms of phantasy and dream. This becomes understandable when he discusses the difference between the significance of universal and individual symbols and when he considers the danger in the interpretation of symbols in the spontaneous art of mental patients.

Concerning the treatment of this schizophrenic girl, Meares points out that a fundamental difference exists between personal and universal symbols:

> "The nature of symbolism is such that any attempt at rule of thumb interpretation is likely to lead to error. A common source of such error is the confusing of universal symbols and individual symbols. The rod, the spear, the snake as phallic symbols, and the hollow-shaped female symbol are the commonplace of Freudian psychology. These are universal sym-bols. They appear as products of the unconscious in all of us, irrespective of race or creed. . . . But in addition to universal symbols, which are common to all mankind, there are other symbols which are created by a particular person, and belong to him and to no one else. These are indi-vidual symbols. They are used by the person to express some particular idea, and they recur with the same meaning in different works of the same person."[33]

This statement concerning the possible fallibility of a therapist's interpre-tation of a patient's symbolism is extremely important and questions the constant intervention of psychoanalysts who tend to give an interpretation of the sym-bolism of their patients' dreams and phantasies only in terms of universal sym-bols and who do not usually encourage their patients to offer their own individual personal interpretations.

On Symbolism as Nonverbal Expression

Although Freud first revealed the role of the unconscious in the interpreta-tion of dreams, he placed specific limitations on such unconscious responses. He described "the dream work is an excellent example of the process occurring in the deeper, unconscious layers of the mind which differ considerably from the familiar, normal processes of thought." He then added, "It also displays a number of archaic characteristics such as the use of a *symbolism* (in this case of a predominantly sexual kind) which it has since been possible to discover in other spheres of mental activity."[34] He then formulated what became an approach to symbolism that has since been regularly followed in the therapeutic methods of all Freudian psychoanalysts.

A concise statement as to the nature of the symbolic process as interpreted by psychoanalysts was amplified by Ernest Jones:

---

[33] Meares, A.: *Op. cit.*, p. 85.

[34] Freud, S.: *Autobiographical Study.* Translated by J. Strachey: New York, W. W. Norton & Co., 1963, pp. 86-87.

"Only what is repressed is symbolized; only what is repressed needs to be symbolized. This conclusion is the touchstone of the psychoanalytical theory of symbolism. Symbolism arises as the result of intrapsychical conflict between the repressing tendencies and the repressed."[35]

This narrow psychoanalytic definition of symbolism ignores the positive role of visual symbolism in the culture of man throughout the ages as a fundamental and normal aspect of human expressions. Such recognition of symbolism as a positive aspect of man's thought and creative expression has already been reviewed in this introduction and stands forth as a natural, positive and normal form of nonverbal, imaged expression shared by both primeval and modern man. Nonverbal expression is the dynamic force behind all creative expression, but it is too little recognized in our therapeutic and educational procedures today. It cannot therefore be considered as related only to the repression of conflicts in its symbolic form.

Aldous Huxley has spoken wisely about the weakness of education on a nonverbal level in a paper on "Human Potentialities." "What is needed," he writes, "if more of the potentialities of more people are to be actualized, is a training on the non-verbal levels of our whole being as systematic as the training now given to children and adults on the verbal level."[35a]

In this statement, Huxley is suggesting the importance of developing nonverbal training in education, but nonverbal training is also much needed in psychotherapy. This is an important aspect of dynamically oriented art therapy, for it encourages nonverbal communication in sessions with the psychotherapist by means of created images, by mental patients.

A leading clinical psychologist, Dr. Robert H. Holt of the Research Center for Mental Health, New York University, has also considered the importance of man's image-making power on the nonverbal level. In his paper, "Imagery: the Return of the Ostracized," Holt recalled the early interest of psychologists in imagery, before and around the twentieth century, and the subsequent decline of interest in the subject. He states, "During the last decade almost all these trends have been reversed, and there are indications that the various types of imagery [which he then lists] will continue to attract more of the psychologists' interest in the future." Although Holt was addressing clinical psychologists, his comments also concern psychoanalysts, because he included them as being involved in neglecting the vital significance of imagery. As Holt writes, "Ironically, psychoanalysis has had as little systematic interest in images as academic psychology."[36]

Holt's comment is closely related to the way in which many psychoanalysts, bound by their verbal techniques, avoid the implications of the symbolic speech of art therapy, which communicates through images. In various forms of psychotherapy it is recognized that the ability to verbalize unconscious conflicts often

[35] Jones, E.: "The Theory of Symbolism." *Papers on Psychoanalysis.* Baltimore, Williams & Wilkins, 1948, p. 116.

[35a] Huxley, A.: "Human Potentialities." *Bull. Menninger Clin.* 25 (No. 2):63-68, 1961.

[36] Holt, R. H.: "Imagery: the Return of the Ostracized." *Amer. Psychol.* 19:263. 1964.

releases bodily tensions and physical symptoms, but much of a patient's personal orientation during psychotherapeutic treatment is expressed nonverbally in the tone of voice, gesture, and images of phantasies and dreams. Also, much of the readjustment of disturbed patients to a more normal life is expressed nonverbally through psychotherapy. Why not then encourage a further step in nonverbal expression through the inclusion of the symbolic speech of art therapy?

IV. HOW DYNAMICALLY ORIENTED ART THERAPY EVOLVED

I have often been asked about my first researches in art therapy begun in 1941 at the New York State Psychiatric Institute. To explain this I must first go back to when I founded and developed the Walden School in 1915 before my first researches in dynamically oriented art therapy with behavior problem children at the Psychiatric Institute.

There were several basic concepts which were implicit in the development of Walden from its inception. The school was established on the basic psychoanalytic insights concerning the importance of the unconscious in education as well as in psychotherapy. A number of artists, writers and professors, as well as some well-known psychoanalysts (such as Dr. A. A. Brill and Dr. Leonard Blumgart), sent their children to Walden and supported its point of view and purpose. Soon, many of the more open-minded teachers undertook personal analyses, and a number of parents with analytic and broad social and artistic interests gave their active support to the pioneering efforts of the Walden School. In its earliest years, besides functioning as an executive and retraining teachers, I directed the spontaneous, free art expression of groups of children. It was then that my deep interest was stirred by the original and amazing images that these young children created from their unconscious. The conviction that such free art expression in children was a symbolic form of speech basic to all education grew stronger as the years passed. I concluded that such spontaneous art expression was also basic to psychotherapeutic treatment.

When I withdrew from Walden, I took time out to write a book on education, *The Child and the World*.[37] It contained a series of dialogues in which various individuals visited a similar school, and the way children reacted under various conditions in a modern school dramatized a search for fundamental values and new techniques to revitalize education.

Some years after I had withdrawn from Walden I was fortunate enough to meet Dr. Nolan D. C. Lewis, who was then the Director of the New York State Psychiatric Institute. In talking with him I found that for many years he had been impressed with the symbolic significance of pictures made by his patients during analysis. I asked him whether he might be interested in an experimental research program in the use of spontaneous art in therapy with some of the behavior-problem children in his hospital. His immediate and sympathetic response to this idea was based on his own experience as to the value of spontaneous art with his own patients.

---

[37] Naumburg, Margaret: *The Child and the World*. New York, Harcourt-Brace, 1928.

The results of my three-year research program in dynamically oriented art therapy with behavior-problem children, that I carried out at the New York Psychiatric Institute with the encouragement and continued interest and support of Dr. Lewis, were published as a book in 1947 with a preface by Dr. Lewis.[38]

The next three years of my work at the Psychiatric Institute were spent in research on the application of art therapy to schizophrenics. Dr. Philip Polatin, Chief of the Women's Division, always supported my work with active encouragement and assistance. The second book on my research at the Psychiatric Institute was on the use of spontaneous art with schizophrenics.[39]

Another case of a schizophrenic patient with whom I worked in art therapy at the Psychiatric Institute was published in Hammer's book, *The Clinical Application of Projective Drawings*.[40]

Following the six years of research at the Psychiatric Institute, I became associated during the next phase of art therapy development with several psychiatric hospitals in New York and Philadelphia. At the same time I began the private practice of art therapy, sometimes alone and sometimes in association with various well-known psychoanalysts and psychiatrists. Because of the growing interest in art therapy, I began the development of my training seminars in "The Techniques and Methods of Art Therapy"; these were given in New York, Philadelphia, Washington and Cambridge.

In 1953 I published a three-year study of a college student treated by means of art therapy—*Psychoneurotic Art: Its Function in Psychotherapy*, with an illuminating preface by Dr. Kenneth E. Appel.[41]

V. DEVELOPMENT OF DYNAMICALLY ORIENTED ART THERAPY IN THE UNITED STATES

Interest in the effectiveness of dynamically oriented art therapy has increased greatly since the writer began her first researches in this area in 1941 at the New York State Psychiatric Institute. Much time was spent in introducing and explaining this new approach to psychiatrists, psychoanalysts, psychologists, art educators and the general public before it was possible in 1958 to establish for graduate students at New York University the first training program which dealt with the principles and methods of dynamically oriented art therapy. During the intervening years, there were invitations to introduce the fundamental concepts of art therapy to various professional groups, through lec-

---

[38] Naumburg, Margaret: *Studies of the "Free" Art Expression of Behavior Problem Children and Adolescents as a Means of Diagnosis and Therapy*. Originally published as Mental and Nervous Disease Monograph #71, 1947. Now distributed by Grune & Stratton, New York.

[39] Naumburg, Margaret: *Schizophrenic Art: Its Meaning in Psychotherapy*. New York, Grune & Stratton, 1950.

[40] Naumburg, Margaret: "Art Therapy: Its Scope and Function," and "Art Therapy with a Seventeen Year Old Schizophrenic Girl." *In* Hammer, E. F.: *The Clinical Application of Projective Drawings*. Springfield, Ill., Charles C Thomas, 1958.

[41] Naumburg, Margaret: *Psychoneurotic Art: Its Function in Psychotherapy*. New York, Grune & Stratton, 1953.

tures and seminars at medical schools and psychiatric hospitals, as well as through exhibits at international congresses, museums and other institutions.[42]

The exhibits of dynamically oriented art therapy at international congresses on adult and child psychiatry have been shown in New York, Montreal, Paris, Zurich and Copenhagen. The writer also had exhibits at a number of the annual meetings of the American Psychiatric Association and has chaired two art therapy symposia at the annual meetings of the American Orthopsychiatric Association. All these approaches have helped to familiarize a wider public with the principles of dynamically oriented art therapy.

As inquiries about how to obtain training in dynamically oriented art therapy increased, it became possible to establish a number of seminars and lectures for qualified students. These took place in psychiatric clinics and hospitals, medical schools, universities, and art and occupational therapy organizations.

The first course introducing the principles and methods of art therapy was introduced in 1958 in the Department of Art Education at New York University. Currently the work continues in the Department of Psychology at the New School in New York City.

As information about the substance of this first introductory course, "Art Education and Personality," became known to graduate students in other departments of New York University, they realized that the course did not deal with the traditional methods of art teaching but rather with the unconscious factors in the development of personality. Increasing numbers began to enroll from the various departments of Psychology, Occupational Therapy, Counseling, Social Work and Special Education.

The original purpose of this beginning course was to supplement the existing program in the Art Education Department by introducing a psychological understanding of the creative process. In the first and second courses emphasis was placed on developing an awareness of the importance of dynamic psychology and on understanding unconscious motivation as it relates to the creative expression of pupils and patients as well as the students themselves.

In order to unify the approach of students from various disciplines who would take the first course, the instructor found it necessary to review many of the basic psychological concepts concerning the unconscious, since a number of students in each class were still unfamiliar with the foundations of dynamic psychology.

The vital role of the unconscious in the responses of pupils, patients or clients, as well as in the students themselves, was examined in order to assist those who had no adequate training in dynamic and abnormal psychology. A number of students in each class had had some form of personal psychotherapy, which made them better able to understand the unconscious conflicts of pupils, clients or patients. It is interesting to note that after taking several of these courses, a number of the students then decided to specialize professionally in art therapy,

---

[42] For example, an exhibition of pictures by the alcoholic woman whose case study begins on page 85 was shown at the Annual Meeting of the American Psychiatric Association in Atlantic City, N. J., May 9-13, 1955.

and quite a few of these students undertook personal psychotherapy in order to better prepare themselves for this new work.

As a means of developing an understanding of the principles of dynamic psychology in students (since it seems so sadly neglected in many of the required undergraduate courses), it has been necessary to demonstrate the role of the unconscious as carried out in various projective techniques. The Rorschach and Thematic Apperception Test, as well as a variety of drawing tests, are shown and discussed in the class. A review of the unconscious factors in the growth and development of the individual from infancy and adolescence to adulthood is then presented in order to show the students how the unconscious plays a vital role in their own lives and the lives of their pupils, patients or clients.

In one of the early sessions in the course, time is allowed for the students to experiment with the "scribble" technique, a practical method of releasing spontaneous images from the unconscious, using large sheets of paper. The scribble technique is explained and demonstrated as a means of freeing repressed and unconscious data from the unconscious. The various pictures created by the class are then placed on the wall, where collectively they help to reveal to the students the great variation in the response of different personalities. The students are quick to observe how many unconscious aspects of their own lives are revealed in their spontaneous designs.

The students are encouraged to fill in the gaps in their own knowledge of dynamic and abnormal psychology, psychiatry and psychoanalysis, as well as the new psychological approaches to the analysis of creativity and symbolism, by spending as much time as possible in using the reading bibliography.

In order to help students understand the profound implications of unconscious expression in the multitude of forms possible in nonverbal speech, pictorial symbolism, in its many manifestations in religion and in ancient cultures, is examined. Various forms of symbolic expression—drawn from such diverse areas as pantomime, drama, myth and ritual—are introduced in order to illumine the range of human symbolic expression. During several sessions, the role of symbolic expression, as released through the unconscious art projections of pupils, patients and clients, is considered and illustrated with slides.

These images projected from the unconscious can only be understood or dealt with adequately by educators and therapists when they have acquired a thorough background in those concepts relating to the unconscious, which have been developed by Freud, Jung, Sullivan, Fromm, Erikson and others. The information thus gained by a survey of various aspects of unconscious responses leads to a deeper understanding of the fact that the difference between normal and abnormal human responses is only a matter of degree, not of kind. Several sessions are spent in discussing these problems, which are illustrated with case studies and slides showing the unconscious emotional responses of behavior-problem children, emotionally disturbed adolescents and adults. One session is spent exploring the personality and the unconscious attitudes of the students as people, whether they are educators, art therapists, psychologists, occupational therapists, or are employed in special education.

In order to prepare students in the class for case study work in the second term's course, "Case Studies of Pupils or Patients Blocked in Creative Expression," the method of preparing a case study in this new field, which includes spontaneous art productions, is discussed and demonstrated. Some of the students are familiar with the usual form of case study as employed for patients in a psychiatric hospital. Such case studies always include a family and personal history, a diagnosis of the patient's illness or emotional problems, and notes on the succession of interviews with patients. These, too, are part of the art therapy case study technique and must be learned by the student. But traditional case histories do not allow for the spontaneous art productions which are included in case histories of patients treated by means of dynamically oriented art therapy.

The students in these courses must, as part of learning the correct form of case study preparation, find out how to interview the pupil or patient and gain the ability to record every spontaneous conversation as it occurs during each art therapy session. Practice in the creation of an actual case study occurs only in the second course. It is especially difficult for educators to acquire the ability to be passive and receptive, for teachers are taught to be active in imparting information to their pupils. The students, whether they be teachers or therapists, must all learn to become passive and receptive, so that they may encourage their pupils or patients to obtain free associations to their projected images. Until students gain in understanding the techniques of interviewing, they will not be able to develop genuine case studies in art therapy.

After interviewing practice, students must be trained to record what pupils or patients say, as well as what is said to them by the therapist. It is sometimes possible, without disturbing a pupil or patient, to jot down in their presence brief notes of the conversation. Notes taken during the art therapy sessions usually tend, however, to impede the free flow of comments by either a pupil or patient. Thus, usually, the entire conversation with the patient should be written down *verbatim*, as soon as possible, following each session, for it is the sequence of these talks that is basic to the therapeutic treatment of pupil or patient by means of art therapy. It is only in the review of these exact written records of what has been spoken during a sequence of sessions that students learn to recognize the dynamic movement and change which is taking place in the treatment of each case. Until the form of a regular case study has become familiar, the way to modify it for the practice of art therapy cannot be developed. In the type of case study used in art therapy, special emphasis is placed on the free associations offered by pupil or patient to the spontaneous pictures produced in their sessions with art educator or therapist.

When the method of organizing a classical case study has been understood, the students are then introduced to the way in which spontaneous images obtained in the process of art therapy are brought into the special form of a case study. Students are shown how the fundamental contribution of Freudian analysis to the technique of "free association" must be understood in order to release the free associations to spontaneous art.

In training students to develop case histories which include spontaneous art productions, it has been necessary to simplify the application of various techniques. When art therapy is to be employed by professionally trained therapists, however, the approach is more complex. Besides encouraging the use of spontaneous art as a means of expressing dreams, phantasies and conflicts, much time is also spent by professional art therapists on verbal communication, as in other types of psychotherapy.

"Case Studies of Pupils or Patients Blocked in Creative Expression"

This course, in the second term, has been conducted in the form of a seminar to which each student brings material as he develops his own case study. The purpose of the course is to help students deal more effectively with pupils or patients who are blocked in spontaneous art expression of their conflicts. Although the emphasis is on a study of a single pupil or patient, the procedures developed in the course help to make students more aware of how to release any inhibited pupil or patient through spontaneous art expression. The students are offered assistance in various visual and verbal techniques for freeing creative expression.

This course is of interest to students in various disciplines. It attracts a number of graduate students in art education and assists them in making their teaching more creative, or it may also lead them to develop more intensive work in art therapy. Clinical and school psychologists have found this course useful in widening the range of their professions, and occupational therapists are coming to recognize that learning to make such case studies with the use of spontaneous art can win them serious recognition from psychiatrists in a hospital setting.

In this case study course, students at each session report on the various stages of the work on their case histories. They begin with the organization of the family and personal history and then learn to make written records of interviews with their pupils or patients. They are next shown how to deal with the spontaneous art productions produced by pupil or patient in each session.

All members of the class, as well as the instructor, discuss whatever data each student presents, and then offer advice and suggestions as to how each case study might be improved. The most difficult problem for many students is learning how to conduct informal interviews with either pupils or patients as a means of encouraging them to express themselves spontaneously about their art productions.

Another aspect of case study training consists of developing in the students an ability to establish rapport and confidence with either the pupil or the patient with whom they are developing their case study. This requires special skill and sensitivity in interviewing. Discussions of the art of interviewing by various authorities are introduced in order to make students aware of the value and importance of the interview method in creating significant case studies based on art therapy.

When the material for a case study, including family history, recorded interviews and a series of pictures has been placed in exact sequence, the final work of organization begins. A careful analysis of the phases of development of pupil or patient in the course of the case study is expected, as well as a summary of what has occurred during the development of the case. This is then followed by a discussion of the insight the student has gained through this new experience.

Advanced Case Study Course

In the second year an advanced case study course continues through two terms for those graduate students who have already taken the introductory case study course. This advanced case study course is also conducted as a seminar which allows free active discussion and exchange among the students and the instructor about the various aspects of their case studies. Students have, from their previous courses, become sufficiently aware of the practical techniques needed for obtaining spontaneous art productions from their pupils or patients, and they now understand how to relate such pictures to the free associations obtained.

The advanced course is always stimulating to the students as well as to the instructor, for the students are able to carry out their reports in many types of case studies. This leads to the development of a broad spectrum of possibilities in the application of dynamically oriented art therapy. A number of students became so interested in the application of art therapy in both education and psychotherapy that they repeated this course from three to six times.

Course for Advanced Clinical Psychologists on Cases of Patients Treated by Means of Art Therapy

In the past, this course has been offered to third and fourth year clinical psychologists at New York University as well as the Workshop for Post Doctoral Clinical Psychologist in Dynamically Oriented Art Therapy. Actual cases of patients treated by means of art therapy have been presented with slides of the art productions of these patients. These included behavior-problem children, schizophrenic, paranoid, alcoholic, depressed, compulsive, obese and ulcer patients. The use of spontaneous art with both individual patients and groups has also been considered.

All these courses and a number of others need to be developed in the near future as part of a complete art therapy training program. It is hoped that regular clinical training for art therapists can soon be established in a psychiatric hospital in New York City, which may lead to a form of official certification.

VI. THE POWER OF THE SYMBOL IN DYNAMICALLY ORIENTED ART THERAPY

The positive value of dynamically oriented art therapy to psychotherapeutic procedures is its recognition of the vital contribution of symbolic images to the practice of psychotherapy. It will, therefore, be important to review the steps of man's cultural heritage which have given emphasis to the image rather than the word. It is necessary to investigate how nonverbal speech by image-making was a vital form of communication in the life of early man. This realization demands a review of how and why man's symbolic projections were translated into the external standards of what today is called "art."

Before we can consider the nature and function of art in its symbolic aspects, we need to be fully aware of the way in which the modern concept of art has been modified by the developments of anthropology and archaeology. In such perspective we therefore include the cave paintings of prehistoric man, the ritual objects of ancient Egyptian and Indian civilizations, as well as the recovered Mayan temples and Cretan palaces, in our efforts to estimate the meaning of man's existence as shown through his art. In the realization that the span of man's creative expression is so unending and so complex, we unwittingly impose our own recent and personal concept of "art" upon those past expressions of man's imaged response to life. In such attempts to evaluate as "art" what our Western culture regards as the significant graphic and plastic productions of the past, we have not taken into account the profoundly different motivation of the peoples of those remote epochs toward their own creative expression. Because ours is an age in which art lacks religious dynamism, we have failed to comprehend the basic motivation of the imaged projections of prehistoric and ancient man. We continue to call such graphic or sculptured expression "art," but to the man of those times, plastic creations served another purpose; he sought through such projections to relate himself to the cosmos and search out the meaning of existence. It has therefore remained impossible for many interpreters today to bridge the motivational gap between the visual expressions of our own day and those of earlier periods. Earlier cultures, which produced anonymous carvings of strange gods and mythical creatures, did so as a gesture of religious dedication, which is not to be confused with "art" in our modern sense. Only when we are able to relinquish temporarily our specialized focus on "art" can we relate ourselves to so different a view of life as is found in certain ancient and primitive cultures.

Whatever interpretation of imaged expression we may give to our "art," we must also realize that man still draws from his unconscious today, as did men of past cultures. Evidence of this is clear in the identical primordial symbols which are found in various parts of the world in the form of rediscovered paintings and modeled shapes.

The well-known art historian and art critic, S. Giedion, in an article, "Transparency, Primitive and Modern," has offered a perceptive analysis of the psychological motives and spiritual aspirations of primeval man.[43] This analysis was made years before his important book, *The Eternal Present: The Beginnings of Art*, was published.[44] In this volume he expanded more completely his conceptions about the similarities of techniques to be found in the art expressions of primitive man and modern artists. Already in his earlier paper, Giedion showed

[43] Giedion, S.: "Transparency: Primitive and Modern." *Art News*, Summer, 1952.
[44] Giedion, S.: *The Eternal Present: The Beginnings of Art*, Bollingen Series XXXV, 6.1. New York, Pantheon Books, 1962.

that the particular psychological responses which were transmitted to us through the art of primeval man, and then lost for eons, did not reappear until recently, when similar techniques in art expression reentered our culture through the revolutionary creations of some of our modern artists. He stated, "Similar methods appear today and at the dawn of art, among others: abstraction, representations of movement, transparency, simultaneity. . . . Going back as far as possible in the realm of art only makes sense when one searches *not to find external likeness, but to compare modes of representations.*"[45]

In order to be receptive to the techniques used by primeval men in their cave paintings, we have to be conscious that for thousands of years art, as known to us and our immediate ancestors, was based on an entirely different tradition. It relied on a naturalistic, descriptive approach. But as Giedion shows in his later volume, *The Eternal Present: The Beginnings of Art*:

> "Primeval art, in contrast to our own directly inherited tradition in art, is never naturalistic. There is no naturalistic art in prehistory.
> ". . . Naturalistic art, as we know it, is an art which imitates the appearance of things, not as they are in reality, but as they appear in one moment from the point of view of a single spectator. This is the effect of perspective for . . . every element in a perspective representation is related to the unique point of view of the individual spectator. Nothing of this sort existed in prehistory."[46]

Giedion elaborates on how primeval art had no vertical nor horizontal relationships, which means it lacked the particular way of seeing which became embedded in our own consciousness thousands of years ago, and whose beginnings were first established in Egyptian art. Our way of looking at things was entirely unknown to primeval man. To him, as Giedion reminds us, "In primeval times, all directions in space had the same value."[47] Not only did primeval man see space as unbounded by vertical and horizontal, according to Giedion, but he showed no sense of time sequence in his art. In such responses he reacted as children do in their drawings and as all of us do in our dream life when the unconscious takes over.

> "Primeval man has a complete freedom of approach to all directional surfaces. That is why, if we wish to come near to an understanding of primeval art, we must strive to free ourselves from the way of looking at things that has been part of our inheritance for thousands of years. The lines and orientation of a prehistoric picture have no relation to the horizontal and vertical."[48]

"What," asks Giedion, "is it that differentiates the space conception of prehistory from that of later periods.?"

---

[45] Giedion, S.: "Transparency: Primitive and Modern." *Op. cit.*, p. 49.
[46] Giedion, S.: *The Eternal Present: The Beginnings of Art*, Bollingen Series XXXV, 6.1. New York, Pantheon Books, 1962, p. 18.
[47] *Ibid.*, p. 91.
[48] *Ibid.*, p. 529.

Gideon comments on four aspects of symbolization by man, from which have grown art, language, myth and science throughout the ages. But what concerns us, primarily, are those of art and language. It is in the fusion of art and language that man has developed his art as a form of symbolic speech; this began in primeval times, came to fruition again in modern art, and is also discoverable today in the art expression of mental patients.

Although Freud has helped to make us aware of the symbolic way that man expresses himself in dreams and other forms of unconscious expression, Giedion has deepened our awareness of the symbolic process by tracing it back to the psychological responses that he recognized in the art of primeval man in his ancient cave paintings.

"Before art man created the symbol. Symbolization arose from the need to give perceptible form to the imperceptible. Symbolization emerged as soon as man had to express the disquieting and intanglible relation . . . first expressed in very primitive ways. The magic symbols that appear most frequently and over the longest periods of prehistory are simple ones. They consist of fragments, the parts standing for the whole; a hand, for example, represents the entire human being, the genitalia represents fertility.

". . . The present revival of interest in the symbol and its meaning leads us back to its origins in prehistory. It is there that the whole process of symbolization can best be studied."[49]

Such a use of a part for a whole symbol by primitive man is exactly what is also found in the symbolic art of schizophrenic patients during art therapy, clear evidence that in all periods of man's development the unconscious remains a basic source of man's creative expression.

Giedion analyzed the three specific techniques that he had found in primeval art: the use of abstraction, transparency and symbolism. These three art techniques first evolved in cave art, were rediscovered by modern artists and now reappear in the art of neurotic and psychotic patients, revealed by means of art therapy, for many of the mental patients have, like modern artists, rediscovered for themselves the immediacy of such techniques as transparency, abstraction and symbolism as a form of visual speech.

Giedion speaks of two types of transparencies used by primeval man: "The first is the superimposition of different configurations—bodies or lines—one over the other. . . . The second way is to make a body transparent, thus portraying its inside and outside simultaneously."[50]

Giedion also points out that many well-known modern artists have rediscovered these techniques and he has shown in his book a number of examples from the work of modern artists to compare with the art of primitive cultures.

Just as Giedion has traced the similarity of techniques to be found in imaged projections in the cave paintings of early man and the creations of

---

[49] *Ibid.*, pp. 78-79.
[50] *Ibid.*, p. 50.

modern artists, G. H. Luquet, the French psychologist, has shown in his books[51] that children today employ, as did primitive man, similar techniques in their imaged expression, drawing elements which they consider essential and omitting others which may not concern them. He also illustrates, with examples, how both child and primitive man also add aspects which, although not visible, are known to be there. The goal then is not "objective realism," but what he calls "mental realism."

This analysis by Luquet of the methods employed in primitive and child art are confirmed by the well-known British art critic, Roger Fry, who in analyzing children's art concluded that the "highly conceptualized vision in children's drawings obtains also in almost all early art."[52]

Since Luquet emphasizes that his "mental realism" includes perception by man's spirit, and since Fry's term, "conceptualized vision," sounds almost too intellectual as a way of describing a child's vision, would not a term like "intuitive actualization" come closer to being an accurate description of such psychological selection, made by both child and primitive in their art projections?

The modern world still remains ignorant of the extent to which ancient cultures were cognizant of the true significance of sex through their sexual practices and symbolic images. This was long before Freud had restored to modern man recognition of the role of unconscious sexual symbolism as expressive of man's hidden conflicts today.

It is necessary, then, to trace the way in which the power of Christian orthodoxy suppressed or distorted those vital truths that existed in sexual symbols in the images left to us by primitive man. Organized Christianity repressed and distorted the original symbolic truths of its own teachings, so that the Christian Church lost touch with the original source of its symbolic inspiration in sexual imagery. A consequence of this schism was the separation of what is now called "art" from its original source in the symbols of all great religions.

A group of nineteenth century investigators uncovered the meaning of sexual symbols in pagan and Christian art and ritual. Since these investigators revealed to a puritanical England, half a century before Freud, that sex symbols transferred from pagan cults were hidden within all Christian art and ritual, they deserve consideration. That these writers lacked understanding of the psychological reasons for the reiteration of sex symbols in so many cultures is evident in their attempt to analyze the symbols, but it was not possible at that time to comprehend the psychological motivation which produced such omnipresent sexual symbolism in ritual and religion until a clearer understanding of the mechanisms of unconscious projection had been reached.

Two British investigators, Payne Knight[53] and Thomas Inman,[54] are representatives of this pre-Freudian exploration of sexual symbols in pagan and

---

[51] Luquet, G. H.: *L'Art Primitif.* Paris, G. Doin & Cre, 1930; *The Art and Religion of Fossil Man* (Tr. J. Townsend Russell, Jr.). New Haven, Conn., Yale University Press, 1930.

[52] Fry, R.: *Last Lectures.* New York, The Macmillan Co., 1939, p. 51.

[53] Knight, R. P.: *An Inquiry into the Worship of Priapus.* London (privately printed), 1865.

[54] Inman, T.: *Ancient Pagan and Modern Christian Symbolism* (4th ed.). New York, Peter Eckler, 1922.

Christian art. Inman, in one of his books on ancient pagan and modern symbolism, includes symbolic designs derived from such ancient cultures as the
Babylonian, Syrian, Hebrew, Hindu, Egyptian, Greek, Roman and early Christian. Writing in the middle of the nineteenth century, he exposes his own Vic-
torianism in the way he handles the forbidden topic of sex:

> "In the following pages the author has felt himself obliged to make
> use of words which are probably only known to those who are more or
> less "scholars." He has to treat of parts of the human body, and acts which
> occur habitually in the world, which in modern times are never referred
> to in polite society but which, in the period when the Old Testament was
> written, were spoken of as freely as we now talk of our hands and feet.
> In those days, everything which was common was spoken of without shame,
> and that which occurred throughout creation, and was seen by everyone
> was as much the subject of conversation as eating and drinking is now.
> The Hebrew writers were extremely coarse in their diction, and although
> this has been softened down by subsequent redactors, much which is in
> our modern judgment improper still remains. For example, where we
> simply indicate the sex, the Jewish historians used the word which was
> given to the symbol by which male and female are known; for example, in
> Gen. 1:27 and V. 2 and in a host of places, the masculine and feminine are
> spoken of as 'zachar' and 'nekebah,' which are best translated as 'borers
> and bored.' "[55]

In tracing the hidden sexual symbols of ancient Hindu and Egyptian art,
Inman explains to the then uninitiated public that the symbol of the eye represents "androgyne creator," shown by the "outer oval as female," and the eyeball
as "the circle" representing "the male lodged therein—i.e., the androgyne creator."
He refers, also, to the significance of "the archway . . . or door, which is symbolic
of the female, like the *vesica piscis*, the oval or the circle."[56]

In showing illustrations of the androgyne Brahma, Inman explains, "It
represents Brahma supreme, who in the act of creation made himself double,
i.e., male and female. In the original, the central part of the figure is occupied
by the triad and the unit, but far too grossly shown for reproduction here. They
are replaced with the *crux ansata*."[57]

The pointed oval form, as a universal symbol of the female, known in
Christian art as the *vesica piscis*, often surrounds the images of the Virgin or
various saints. Inman, in order to describe this form, explains its symbolic truth
as referring to "the feminine element in creation." This symbol, he says, could
be found in "designs which naughty youths so frequently chalk upon walls to
the disgust of the proper part of the community."

Inman reviewed the manner in which pagan symbols have permeated
Christian worship and therefore convinced himself that Christian doctrine "is
simply horrible—blasphemous and heathenish." He writes:

---

[55] *Ibid.*, p. xxx.
[56] *Ibid.*, pp. 7-8.
[57] *Ibid.*, p. 9.

*"I cannot help regarding the sexual element as the key which opens
almost every lock of symbolism* [italics mine], and however much we may
dislike the idea that modern religionists have adopted emblems of an
obscene worship, we cannot deny the fact that it is so, and we may hope
that with a knowledge of their impurity we shall cease to have a faith
based upon a trinity and virgin—a lingam and a yoni."[58]

André Malraux, the French writer and politician, in considering the irrational and dream element in modern art, refers to the "diabolical destructive
principle" found "in the demons of Babylon, of the early Church and the
Freudian subconscious" which "all have the same visage. And the more ground
the new devils gain in Europe, the more her art tends to draw on earlier cultures
which, too, were plagued by their contemporary demons." To make his point
that a faith reaching beyond personal artistic expression is the source of great
art, Malraux cites Goya, who, he states, "foreshadows all modern art: nevertheless painting in his eyes is not the supreme value; its task is to cry aloud the
anguish of man forsaken by God. The seemingly picturesque elements are
linked up . . . as the great Christian art was linked with faith . . . with certain
deep-rooted collective emotions, which modern art has chosen to ignore. . . .
The fantastic in his work does not stem from albums of Italian capricci, but
from the underworld of man's fears."[59]

This is a valuable pronouncement, even though Malraux assumes that the
way for modern man to rejuvenate his art is through a return to Christian faith.
Neither Malraux nor those psychoanalysts who look forward to curbing the
irrational element in man show sufficient faith in the transformative power of
man's unconscious. While the unconscious contains destructive and fearful
forces which some religionists and psychoanalysts warn against, the unconscious
is also the source of that generative power which makes it possible for art to
become a means of integration and renewal to the human psyche.

Sexual symbolism in primitive and non-Christian art often has been misunderstood and distorted. To the primitive, sex symbols were not something to
be decried or feared. They represented for him a positive and universal life-
giving force in the cosmos and in man. In much anthropological research this
attitude of primitive peoples is evident.

The recurrent use of universal symbols relating to the creative principle in
the cosmos and in the individual life of man, as personified in the imaged projection of sexual symbols, is significant. It is not surprising that in man's efforts to
express his relation to the universe and to his own experience we find the same
life symbols in the unconscious of contemporary man as of primitive and ancient
man.

Although we see the use of sexual and other human symbols throughout the
ages of man's creative projections, we are not in a position to know, but only to
speculate about, what such symbolic expression may have meant to early man
in those primitive or ancient cultures that have now passed away. From artifacts

----

[58] *Ibid.*, p. 101.
[59] Malraux, A.: *Voices of Silence.* New York, Doubleday, 1953.

and ritual objects, as from stone tablets and papyri, archaeologists and anthropologists have helped to reconstruct forgotten and long-buried cultures. But the interpretations of modern man as to the meaning of the symbolic remains of ancient societies are based on the ideas, beliefs, and prejudices of our own different culture. We can only speculate about the total purpose of remote priapic or mystery rites. Important as is the insight gained from the psychoanalytic approach to symbolism, especially to sexual symbols, it cannot reproduce all aspects of the ancient significance of such symbols to primitive man or to ancient cultures not rooted in the Western tradition. It is therefore of considerable interest to supplement the psychoanalytic approach to sexual symbols with that of a still-surviving primitive culture like that of the Maori.

In a little-known but fascinating volume, *Maori Symbolism*, a Maori, Hohepa Te Rake, described and interpreted the meaning of the culture and sacred legends of his people. He came to the conclusion that since Western scientists had been able to uncover the inner meaning of some Maori symbolism and because his own Maori culture was dying, it was his obligation and duty to explain the true meaning of the long-withheld secret teachings of the Maori tradition. What he has revealed in this book has been delineated by means of various modes of symbolic expression, such as movement, gesture, carving and tattooing.

In the interpretation of Maori symbolism his reporter, Ettie A. Rout, explains:

> "When we speak of Maori art, it must be understood that we speak of Maori Symbolism. There was no art apart from Symbolism . . . that is, there was no such thing as Art for Art's sake. The carving was not sculpture in the European sense at all; it was writing and expression of ideas and principles. . . . The twin ideals of Ancient Maori life were Beauty and Duty, but Beauty must be expressed through the performance of the Duty of cultivation. On this Religion of Cultivation and its Symbolism the whole of Maori Life and Art was based.
>
> "The male and female life symbols are hidden within the arabesque carvings on the rafters of the sacred Maori houses; they were always present but partially disguised . . . It was the duty of the artist to conceal as well as reveal: the Sacred Symbol was to be the foundation of the pattern. . . . Usually only half is represented: or half the male and half the female (symbol) are combined. Maori jade Tiki . . . are symbolic ornaments representing the Immortality of the Race and the means of achieving it. They are composed entirely of the male and female life symbols and sacred beaks carved in the form of the phallus."[60]

In the Maori designs of sacred life the symbols are clearly representative of the male and female principles. The oval or elliptical forms are a universal symbol familiar in both Eastern and Western cultures. When this oval form appears in Christian art as a surround of the Virgin or the Christ figure, it is

---

[60] Rout, Ettie A.: *Maori Symbolism*. New York, Harcourt-Brace, 1926, pp. xxx-xxxi.

known as the *vesica piscis*. The ovoid form of the *vesica piscis*, representing the vagina, might contain the configuration of the Christ child represented as part of the pregnant Virgin Mary.

A use of the sex symbols similar to their usage in Maori art and Christian iconography has been found in a number of unconscious symbolic designs of mental patients in art therapy. A specific example is the spontaneous art of an emotionally disturbed college girl who made a symbolic image in which both the male and female principles were represented in the same combined form as is found in Maori carvings.[61] This technique of "transparency" is found also in child art and is favored as well by modern artists as a method of translating "what the spirit knows" rather than "what the eye sees."

The well-known Freudian analyst, Franz Alexander, considered that the goal of integration for the human psyche of the artist, as well as of other men, depends on an acceptance of what he emphasizes as the "reality" of the world of the senses;[62] this concept typical of deterministic psychoanalysis demands a rational control of the irrational or mystical aspects of the emotional life of man.

To confirm his point that healthy art depends on an acceptance of the actual external world, Alexander cites the Impressionist movement. Since Impressionist pictures, as Alexander understands them, deal with the outer world of landscapes and people, he therefore assumes that Impressionist methods depict the concrete reality of existence. But those contemporaries who rejected the Impressionists criticized them for not presenting what the public of that time considered as reality, and that same audience scorned the vision of the Impressionists as presented in their scientific fragmentation of color. Similarly, the abstractionists of today have been attacked as failing to represent the reality of the visible external world.

When the analyst makes the senses the means of measuring what he calls "reality," does he not ignore the "something behind appearances" which intensifies reality? This added factor includes "mental realism" as defined by Luquet, as well as the inner contemplation of the Eastern artist or the Christian mystic; all these approaches lead to a nonliteral presentation which has the quality of a reality that includes, but reaches beyond, the physical senses.

Psychoanalysis has made both the artist and the general public increasingly aware of the fact that man's unconscious thinks and feels in symbolic images. It has shown most clearly that intellectualization and the exaggerated verbalism of our culture have been imposed on the deeper and more primitive levels of our unconscious mode of imaged expression. That the primary method of unconscious projection in man deals with pictorial images was first explained by Freud in relation to his study of dreams.

Although Freud did not emphasize the use of drawing in psychoanalytic treatment, it has in recent years become recognized as a fruitful mode of exploring the imaged projections of the unconscious. Dynamically oriented art therapy

---

[61] Naumburg, Margaret: *Psychoneurotic Art: Its Function in Psychotherapy.* New York, Grune & Stratton, 1953, p. 74.

[62] Alexander, F.: "The Psychoanalyst Looks at Art." *Explorations in Psychoanalysis.* New York, Julian Press, 1953.

has become possible as a consequence of Freud's achievement in recording the psychological mechanisms of unconscious response in man. So fundamental have been his revelations of human motivation that both psychologists and the general public have adopted the analytic concepts of projection, sublimation, identification, condensation, etc., as a current expression of the way man thinks and speaks today. Although the layman may not understand the deeper significance of these psychological mechanisms, he has come to accept the validity of the unconscious in his life. At the same time, the contemporary artist has made his own use of the dynamism of the unconscious and its symbolic content as revealed by psychoanalysis.

Through improved technics, psychoanalysis has become increasingly aware of the unconscious mental processes of psychotics. Freud originally considered psychotics untreatable, but a growing number of schizophrenic and manic-depressive patients are now being successfully treated by psychoanalysts. This means that psychotic behavior, once considered as totally bizarre and senseless, is now perceived to be a form of symbolic communication from the unconscious which it is possible to decipher. It is therefore inaccurate to dismiss the projections of a psychotic as being without meaning, as did Malraux in his *Voices of Silence.* Psychiatry now recognizes that no gesture, facial expression, jumbled phrase nor strange design projected by a psychotic is meaningless. All such projections are charged with specific symbolic significance, whether they are comprehensible or not to another person, for it is now known that disturbed patients are not merely talking to themselves but attempting to communicate with others by little understood means.

The kind of symbolism chosen by man in his visual projections from prehistory until the present has certain strikingly similar elements. The archaic patterns projected from the unconscious imagery of man today are rooted in the same human responses as those which motivated man in primitive times, for age-old patterns of symbolic response remain active and observable today.

We have seen what art critics and psychologists have noted about different stages of cultural development: that whenever inner experiences have been projected by man into nonrealistic images, their creators tend to use similar techniques. We have realized that such technical methods of expression, discovered spontaneously in different epochs, are found to include (1) the use of abstraction as a means of expressing inner realizations, (2) the use of simultaneity of focus rather than perspective, (3) the intensification of the dynamics of movement by means of distorted line, and (4) the use of "transparency" or overlaid images to depict what the mind knows to exist, rather than what the eye actually sees.

The expansion of psychoanalysis has led the general public to become increasingly aware that the unconscious speaks in symbolic images. However, one of the first French psychiatrists to note the sexual symbols in the drawings of his "insane" patients was Max P. Simon, who was also shocked by such "obscene drawings" and ordered the patient to cease making them.[63]

---

[63] Simon, M. P.: "Les ecrits et les dessins des alienés." *Arch. Anthrop. Crim.* (Paris) 3:318-355, 1888.

Since the discoveries of psychoanalysis concerning the dynamics of the unconscious as well as the recognition of the symbolic art of prehistoric cultures and ancient civilizations, new perspectives have been given to the meaning and value of unconscious elements in the symbolic aspects of all art. We know now that distortion, for instance, may be due to purposeful emphasis, not to ignorance or pathology. We can also recognize that simultaneity of focus in a head by Picasso or primitive man, although differing from external appearance, may nevertheless intensify an inner meaning. Acceptance of such direct and simultaneous expression of multiple aspects of human or other forms is conclusive confirmation of the significance of recurrent symbolic imagery in man's art, for in such projections—whether made by the primitive, the child or the modern artist—there are, in the choice and arrangement of these nonliteral, universally valid formulations, certain deep psychological laws at work.

Giedion has pointed out how modern artists, from their own psychological needs, rediscovered techniques that were used by primitive and ancient man: "When the contemporary artist tries to seize hold of some particles of his inner life, he also tries to turn his eyes inward,"[64] as did primeval man.

Jean Arp, the French painter, sculptor and poet, after being shown examples of primeval art wrote to Giedion in reference to his own spontaneous experience in creating transparencies:

> "Now, under lowered lids, the inner movement streams untainted to the hand. In a darkened room it is even easier to follow the guidance of the inner movement than in the open air. A conductor of inner music, the greater designer of prehistoric images, worked with eyes turned inwards. So his drawings gain in transparency; open to interpenetration, to sudden inspiration, to recovery of the inner melody, to the circling approach, and the whole is transmitted into one great exhalation."[65]

Giedion also states: "Picasso expressed the direct projection of the inner light which commands the artist's hand: 'If you paint, close your eyes and sing,' he said."[65a]

Giedion has shown how the use of transparencies in cave paintings is also to be found in the work of such modern artists as Arp, Klee and others. He also illustrates this with reproductions of the work of these artists and of the art of the cave painters, showing how modern artists employ the technique of transparency in the same way as primitive man. The use of transparency is to be found also in many of the pictures created by mental patients treated by means of dynamically oriented art therapy. An example of such use of transparency is shown in the case study of a depressed woman of 55 who drew a picture of "Four Generations" in which her mother, herself, her daughter and grandson were all drawn with their red hearts showing through their nude bodies. (See p. 157.) Another drawing containing the use of transparency was

---

[64] Giedion: *The Eternal Present: The Beginnings of Art.* P. 55.
[65] *Ibid.*
[65a] *Ibid.*, p. 56.

made by a schizophrenic girl in the course of treatment by means of dynamically oriented art therapy. This design revealed the fetal form of a child within a womb.[66]

In primeval art sexual symbolism represented by the female form is universalized to express the fertility aspect of the woman, while in the art of mental patients the sexual symbolism is generally personal and tends to express the resolution of some deep sexual conflict that relates either to a possibly distorted relation to a parent of either sex or, on occasion, to the final acceptance in unification of the split in the human psyche, as it relates to both its masculine and feminine components. An example of such an unconscious split in the psyche of a schizophrenic patient was made in a double-faced sculptured form created in a semitrance state.[67] She first created a female face with the head covered with a snood. Turning the figure around, she created a male face on the back of the head. When she realized what she had done, she would have destroyed it if her attention had not been drawn to something else.

Symbolic art was brought to the attention of the modern public by the Surrealists. The Surrealists introduced the cultivation and permissive release of unconscious content in their art. The publicizing of psychoanalysis undoubtedly influenced the development of such expression by responsive artists. The concurrent work of such artists has included a growing interest in the irrational in phantasy and dream images, increased use of distortion and archaic forms of expression, substitution of a part for the whole, the use of transparency, and the development of multiple instead of unified focus. These and a number of other methods found in the expression of modern symbolic art have received contradictory interpretations as to their meaning from both art critics and psychoanalysts. It must not be forgotten, however, that these techniques apply also to the art of mental patients; this signifies, as already suggested by Giedion, that such techniques are a universal heritage of man throughout the ages.

In the case material which follows, the actual facts of each patient's personal and family history have of course been disguised, but not in a way to interfere with the essentials of each case.

---

[66] Naumburg, Margaret: *Psychoneurotic Art: Its Function in Psychotherapy.* P. 26, 3d.
[67] Naumburg, Margaret: *Schizophrenic Art: Its Meaning in Psychotherapy.* Pp. 170, 171.

FOREWORD TO THREE CASE STUDIES
ILLUSTRATING THE THEORY AND PRACTICE
OF DYNAMICALLY ORIENTED ART THERAPY

The following three studies of emotionally disturbed women illustrate various ways in which the process of art therapy can function in the treatment of such conditions as deep depression, ulcer and alcoholism, for the art therapy approach is based on the recognition that every individual has a latent capacity to project his inner conflicts into visual form. Neither the alcoholic woman nor the depressed patient described in this volume had drawn or painted prior to the art therapy sessions. In the first case, an ulcer patient who was a professional artist, the problem was quite different. This woman had been unable to paint for six years before undertaking art therapy, and she found that art therapy was useful both as a form of treatment and as a means of freeing her ability to paint again. When the alcoholic and depressed patients began to draw for the first time, they both discovered that they were able to say in pictures what they had never been able to reveal through words.

The procedures of art therapy proved flexible enough, in the treatment of the three women whose cases are considered in this book, to be readily adjusted to the different individual needs of these very different types of emotional disturbance. The range and variety of the original art productions of all three patients illustrate the way in which the unconscious can be released into spontaneous images.

To the alcoholic woman, art therapy offered a genuine channel of expression for her hallucinations and phantasies. For the depressed woman, art therapy lent itself to the release of long-repressed and tragic life experiences, and it offered a method of recovering repressed memories of her childhood and adult life through her growing power of original creative expression. The experience of art therapy helped to release the ulcer patient from both her painful past and her still critical present, so that she renewed and expanded the creative promise of her own artistic gift, which had been for many years inhibited by unresolved conflicts.

I. ART THERAPY IN THE TREATMENT OF AN ULCER PATIENT, A PROFESSIONAL ARTIST

This study concerns the use of analytically oriented art therapy in the treatment of a 42-year-old Canadian woman, who will be known as Mrs. Felix. In an exploratory session she explained that she sought treatment by means of art therapy because (1) she wanted help in breaking up her second marriage; (2) she needed assistance in overcoming her own block in creative expression as a professional portrait painter; and (3) since she was an artist-teacher in a mental hospital, she wished practical training in the principles and practice of art therapy.

She was told that such varied and complex expectations could not be dealt with simultaneously, that she must first begin with her own psychotherapy and then with insight gained through her own treatment she could later (if she so desired) work professionally with her patients in the hospital. Mrs. Felix, an intelligent and sensitive woman, responded to this advice and accepted the necessity of beginning with her personal therapy. Like many other artists when they first enquired about possible treatment by means of art therapy, she became anxious as to whether such treatment might not interfere with her own creativity. She was assured that analytically oriented art therapy encouraged the release of spontaneous images from the unconscious as a form of symbolic speech, and that such pictures became an aid in releasing unconscious conflicts. The practice of art therapy, it was explained, supplements the verbal techniques basic to most forms of psychotherapy today.

PLAN OF THE SESSIONS

Since Mrs. Felix would have to commute between Montreal and New York, the art therapy sessions were arranged for alternate weekends each month, with two 2-hour sessions on each trip. The therapy sessions of the first year were somewhat irregular and intermittent, and there were only 56 sessions.

During the second year, covering a period of eight months, there were 20 sessions. This meant that over a period of 19 months there were 76 sessions, equivalent to about 140 hours of therapy.

In the summer of the first year, in the ninth month of therapy Mrs. Felix suspended sessions for six weeks, contrary to the therapist's advice. Then an emotional crisis brought her back to therapy. In the second year, there had been marked improvement in the patient's adjustments with her husband and children as well as in her professional work, but the patient would frequently cancel sessions, because of either family responsibilities or resistance to dealing with her conflicts. Such interruptions made it difficult to sustain adequate therapeutic contacts.

THE PATIENT'S HISTORY

Mrs. Felix was 42 years old and had been married twice. Her first husband was 11 years older than herself and the second husband was 12 years older. After some months of therapy, Mrs. Felix, in reviewing the pattern of the men in her life, was able to say, "I tried to marry my father and got a son. All these men, including my two husbands and my present lover, were first dependent on their mothers and then on me."

There were no children by her first marriage. The patient had always been eager to have children and had been a devoted mother to the boy and two girls of the second marriage. The conflicts of her present marriage, as well as the relation to the lover, are dealt with in relation to the unconscious projections of her pictures.

Early Family History

In the first therapy sessions the patient told of spending an extremely happy life with both her parents when she was young. In adolescence she was especially close to her father because of their shared intellectual interests. When she grew up and wanted to study art, her mother encouraged this wish, but her father objected and wanted her to become a writer. She then spoke of the continuing warm and intimate relation with her mother, which lasted until her mother's death some time after Mrs. Felix's second marriage.

Later in the therapy her image of the relation to her mother as a child and adult was remarkably different. She recalled that besides her beautiful and petite red-haired mother, a niece of her mother's (who was about the patient's age) lived with them. This cousin had auburn-colored hair and was beautiful like the mother, and Mrs. Felix grew up under the shadow of these two more attractive women. The patient felt femininely inadequate and unable to compete in attracting men. One painful childhood memory concerned the mother's vanity in trying to force the patient's feet into shoes a size too small for her. She also recalled that, first, the cousin and later the mother took away her various beaux, forcing her to be satisfied with the second-best boys. To this, she attributed her later insatiable desire for more and more beaux, in order to prove that she was really well-liked.

The pattern of the patient's early adult life was clearly that of carrying more than her share of responsibility in earning money, not only to support herself but also to help her parents financially so as to gain their approval. Only months later was the patient, during therapy, able to become more critical of her idealized image of the mother. In contrast to her recollection of her mother as beautiful and glamorous, the patient recalled herself as very prim in appearance and unable to live up to her mother's expectations. The mother frequently reminded Mrs. Felix that because of her looks she would never marry and must therefore decide on a career. In the course of therapy the patient began to see that the mother's support of her desire to study art had a practical motivation rather than a sympathetic one.

During therapy the patient's first recollections of the father concerned her wonderful intellectual companionship with him as they shared reading Shakespeare and other writers. Then followed painful memories of how the father had unjustly punished her when she was young. She then recalled how, during her adolescence, her father became jealous of her boyfriends.

Recollections of Two Unsatisfactory Marriages

Between sessions Mrs. Felix wrote down much of her life history, in which she wondered why she had married men so much older than herself. Both husbands, she observed, were sexually passive. In both marriages she said that "the pull between dependence and independence is one that I have never been able to come to terms with."

Divorce from First Husband and Consequent Breakdown

The failure of Mrs. Felix's first marriage had reinforced her childhood sense of guilt and inadequacy. Following her divorce, Mrs. Felix at 34 was hospitalized for a duodenal ulcer. She remained in the hospital for three weeks on a milk diet. There was no hemorrhage nor perforation. For a year she continued on a convalescent ulcer diet, but the ulcer was not reactivated. Pyloric spasms occurred now and then when the patient was disturbed but there were no new craters since the original ulcer. It is significant that the patient recalled that prior to these ulcer symptoms her only childhood illnesses related to what she termed "stomach disturbances."

The struggle between wishing to be independent while also needing dependence runs through the entire pattern of Mrs. Felix's professional and love life. It is therefore important to quote, briefly, from Franz Alexander's penetrating description of the ulcer patient, which is applicable to Mrs. Felix's responses. Her pictures made during the art therapy sessions confirm Alexander's description of the excessive dependency of the ulcer patient. Mrs. Felix's designs form a pictorial map of the ulcer process or pattern. As Alexander analyzes the response of the ulcer patient:

"The wish to remain in the dependent infantile situation—to be loved and cared for—was in conflict with the adult ego's pride and aspiration for independence, accomplishment, and self-sufficiency. . . . In the depth of his personality the patient with an ulcer has an unconscious longing for the sheltered existence of a little child. He carefully hides his dependent attitude from himself, however, and represses it so that it cannot find expression in overt behavior, in his personal relations. The repressed longing for love is the unconscious psychological stimulus directly connected with the physiological processes leading finally to ulceration."[1]

The Second Marriage

During the first year of art therapy Mrs. Felix introduced a number of significant allusions to the inadequacy of her sex relations with her second husband, and frequently referred to the husband's lack of masculinity. At the end of the first year of therapy, the therapist, while reviewing Mrs. Felix's pictures, reminded her of some of her previous references to her husband's young men friends. Mrs. Felix then denied emphatically that such episodes implied homosexual tendencies in her husband. At that time the possibility of the husband's inversion was more than Mrs. Felix could yet face. Were she to admit this possibility, it would have been an immediate threat to her marriage. Four years later, however, long after therapy had ceased, Mrs. Felix telephoned the therapist to say that convincing proofs of the husband's homosexuality had now determined her to seek a divorce.

Crisis in the Second Marriage

In her first session, Mrs. Felix had spoken of the severe emotional conflicts in her second marriage, which had reached their climax at the time of the birth of her third child some six years before she came for therapy. She had then been hospitalized because of a deep depression. Her recovery, she added, had been helped by some psychoanalytic treatment. But in this first interview with the art therapist, she was not yet able to admit that at the time of her hospitalization she had attempted to kill herself by slashing her wrists. Unable to face the truth about her husband, she had then escaped into depression and tried halfheartedly to commit suicide. While she was hospitalized, she emphasized that the lover had been more concerned than her husband about her own condition and that of the newborn infant.

The Lover

The lover, who appears in a number of her pictures (not shown), had during many years played a serious emotional role in Mrs. Felix's life. When she first asked the therapist for assistance in breaking up her second marriage, she said that she looked forward to "spending my middle age in peace and happiness married to my lover." She added that both she and the lover would first have to untangle their present marriages. However, since the lover repeatedly postponed getting his divorce, Mrs. Felix would then revert to extreme dependence on her husband.

---

[1] Alexander, F.: *Psychosomatic Medicine.* New York, W. W. Norton & Co., 1950.

THE ART THERAPY SESSIONS

During the first 19 months of therapy, Mrs. Felix made some 80 pictures and small "doodle" drawings. Twenty-three of the most significant of these designs will be shown in the sequence in which they were created. They reveal the basic conflicts of the patient, which correspond so clearly to the psychological responses of the typical ulcer patient.

During the following three years Mrs. Felix's therapy sessions continued intermittently. In only 20 of the later sessions did she make any pictures. In the other sessions she dealt verbally with her dreams and her conflicts.

Introduction to the Patient's Pictures

Mrs. Felix's pictures vividly represent the nature of her unconscious conflicts before she recognized their significance. In addition to her large drawings and paintings, some tiny "doodle" drawings would appear. These usually dealt with long-repressed fears and memories.

"Myself Surrounded by Ice": from a Dream.*

Mrs. Felix made this painting (Fig. 1) at home after the preliminary interview. She explained it as:

> "A woman—myself—but it's a symbolic figure lying face downward. The scene is the North Pole. All around is ice with a shimmering blue edge. The woman's knees seem to be drawn up at her middle as if she were holding them to her. At her middle is a rich red, deep and warm and beautiful. I think I have this warmth and nobody knows it. I give the impression of being cold. The picture made me sad. . . . This is the way I appear to my husband. Certainly I keep myself from showing any feeling when I'm with him. Why can't I be nicer to him even though I no longer expect anything from him as a husband? If I were really free I could." (The patient was no longer having sex relations at this time with the husband.)

Mrs. Felix was not aware of how clearly she had projected her own illness in this painting, for the blood-red mass was symbolic of her bleeding ulcer. That this blood splotch represented an unconscious ulcer symbol was not then interpreted to the patient, for art therapy encourages the patient to gradually uncover the meaning of his own symbolic productions. In relation to this self-portrait, Mrs. Felix referred to her husband's accusations about her sexual inadequacy in their marriage, and she spoke of her feeling of guilt about having failed in both her marriages. She was then overwhelmed by a sense of being victimized by life.

"Odalisque: Myself as a Glamorous Female"

In this second painting (Fig. 2) drawn a month later, Mrs. Felix immediately identified this figure as herself. "Here, again," she said, "is my longing for the fulfillment of womanhood; here are the heavy breasts, the voluptuous pose."

---

* Titles to pictures given by the patients are in quotation marks.

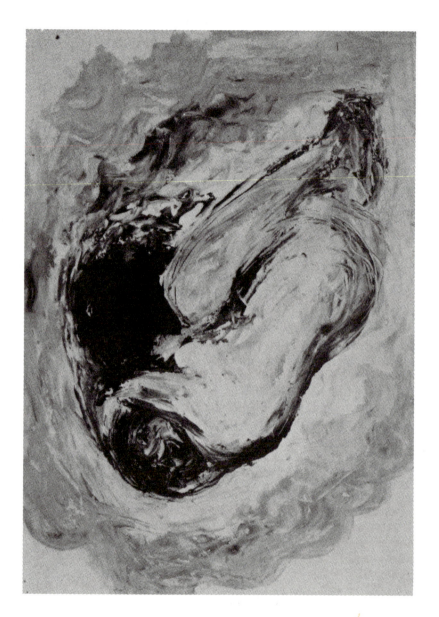

Fig. 1.   "Myself Surrounded by Ice": from a Dream.

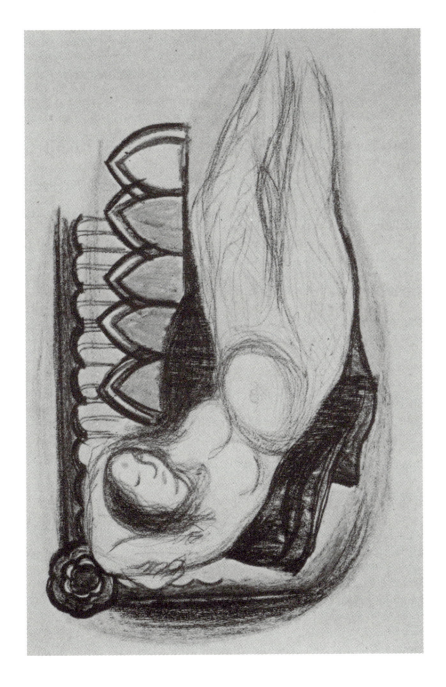

Fig. 2.   "Odalisque: Myself as a Glamorous Female."

She is now, at the beginning of therapy, presenting herself as longing to be glamorous and sensual so as to compete with her attractive mother and cousin. "The picture is suggestive," she added, "of my own divided feelings, which are confused. I want to do more drawings and less talking."

The patient's longing to be glamorous relates to her failure to compete successfully with her beautiful red-haired mother and her teen-aged cousin who lived with them. In contrast, the patient had dark hair and felt that these two women considered her prim and plain. Throughout her life Mrs. Felix said she lived out this competitive feeling by never being satisfied with the many men who found her attractive.

In the first sessions the patient had described her warm and close relation to the mother, who had encouraged her study of art when the father opposed it and wished her to become a writer. But as therapy proceeded, recollections of her idealized image of her sympathetic relation to the mother broke through. She recalled that her mother tried to force her as a child to wear shoes that were too small for her. Later she remembered that both her cousin and her mother had, as she grew up, stolen her beaux from her so that she had to be satisfied with second best.

"A Clown" was Mrs. Felix's next picture, drawn a few days later. It is not shown because of its resemblance to the lover. She said, "It expresses my mixed feelings about him—contempt for his weakness and his immature playboy attitude." Although the lover continued talk of sharing his future with Mrs. Felix, he died some years later without ever attempting to divorce his wife.

Broken Tree: a Dream

This picture (Fig. 3) was brought from home at this time by Mrs. Felix, who explained, "It drew itself. It suggests a particular evening I spent with a man I was in love with, which broke up unhappily, before I'd been married. Everything in this picture hurts, and yet as I look, it is not deeply violent. The landscape with the 'blasted oak' is hackneyed. I feel that I hurt myself on the rocks. The moon is my injured womanhood."

The Phallic Mother: Based on an Earlier Dream

This meticulously developed small oil painting (Fig. 4), which Mrs. Felix brought to a session in the second month, shows the skilled craftsmanship of a professional painter. Previously the patient had only emphasized her warm and companionable relation to her mother. She was now both shocked and surprised at this disparaging mother image which broke through from her unconscious. The carefully painted red bangs and hair were, she said, like her mother's. The high-necked lace dress suggested the style of collars worn by her mother and grandmother. The horrible, long, grey-green face of the mother recalled a previous dream in which she had seen the mother's face with male genitalia hanging from it. In this picture, she explained, the long hanging chin was the substitute symbol of the penis. Afraid to admit the full import of her original phallic mother dream, she had in this picture displaced the penis upward into the face.

Fig. 3.   Broken Tree: a Dream.

Only months later did she recognize the real meaning of this design when she painted another picture of the "Elephant and Shark" ten months later.

Two Pencil Doodles of Mother and Child (The first transference images)

These two tiny pencil doodles (Figs. 5a and 5b) were drawn with five others two months later on the patient's flight to New York. Frequently, before arriving for an appointment Mrs. Felix would scribble small doodles which revealed feelings that she was trying to repress. These doodle drawings, she explained, represented herself as a child nursing at the mother-therapist's breast. The therapist is represented as the Good Mother who fed her. In the second doodle picture the patient, as the child, is rejected. Here is Mrs. Felix's first imaged projection of her "transference" to the therapist, as both the Good Mother and the Bad Mother. Sandor Rado has analyzed such ambivalence toward the mother in depressive patients. The patient's two suicidal attempts identify her as a depressive type.

Fig. 4.   The Phallic Mother: Based on an Earlier Dream. Color plate on page x.

The split between the "good" and "bad" mother in Mrs. Felix's doodles represents, according to Rado, how the child's early responses to the mother expressed either pleasure or pain. This depends on:

> ". . . whether she caresses her child with a happy smile or is angry and disregards or even hurts it. It is easy for us to say that it is one and the same mother in two different moods . . . at first . . . he is still wholly dominated by the pleasure principle, and he distinguishes between these two impressions as objects which are 'good' or 'bad,' or as we may say, as

his 'good mother' or his 'bad mother.' . . . As soon as the child comes under the influence of a strong love-impulse his whole real knowledge about the bad side of his mother is simply blotted out; and, conversely, when his hate impulses break through, there is nothing in the mother who is now 'bad' to remind him that this mother is also wont to be good."[2]

Introducing the Scribble Technique

For the first time it was now possible, in the third month of therapy, to get the patient to experiment freely with what is called the scribble technique (see p. 61). It is more difficult for a trained artist, as in the case of Mrs. Felix, to relax sufficiently to allow the unconscious to express itself in the unexpected forms and symbols released through the scribble technique.

Fig. 5a.   Fig. 5b.
Two Pencil Doodles of Mother and Child (The first transference images).

Abstract Design (Scribble)

Mrs. Felix was amazed and delighted as this abstract design (Fig. 6) developed from her first attempted scribble. It gave her special satisfaction because she recognized that for the first time she was beginning to let unconscious expression break through spontaneously. Since she had always been a realistic painter, she was especially interested in developing her new ability to create abstract design. She therefore proposed taking home this abstract scribble design in order to develop it into a serious painting. It was necessary to explain to Mrs. Felix that if she capitalized too quickly on this first free outpouring of

[2] Rado, S.: "Problems of Melancholia." *Int. J. Psychoanal.* 9:431-432, 1928.

her unconscious in a scribble she would block the spontaneous release of her unconscious through the art therapy procedure. When she understood the importance of these unconscious pictures as the basis of the art therapy approach, she willingly postponed elaboration of her immediate designs. She was assured that on the completion of therapy she could use her pictures in any way that she wished.

"Devil": an Unconscious Symbol of the "Bad" Mother (Scribble)

This design (Fig. 7), derived from a "scribble," was called "Devil" by Mrs. Felix. It was made soon after her previous Abstract Design. "I made it after a bad stomach attack, which followed an upset in the household," she said. "I see a similarity in this fierce devil face to the mother in my first doodle of 'Bad Mother and Child' (Fig. 5b). This devil is trampling on something."

The patient did not finish this picture, saying that she was fearful of making it into "too artistic a design," but it was evident to the therapist that the picture really remained unfinished because Mrs. Felix became frightened at the degree of hostility she had again released against the mother. It took seven more months before she was able to express her violent hostility against her mother in a picture in which the mother was projected as a fierce-jawed wolf who was suckling the patient as a baby (see Fig. 13).

Double Fetal Form (Scribble)

Here (Fig. 8) is one of the many scribble images made by the patient to express her longing to withdraw from life's conflicts by returning to the womb.

First Dream : the Bull Represents the Sexual Threat of the Father

When Mrs. Felix showed these paintings of her two bull dreams to the therapist (drawn two months after the Double Fetal Form), she said that they were the first in which she had dealt with her relation to her father. After creating the first bull design (Fig. 9a), she explained that it recalled to her a disturbing sexual episode with her father during her adolescence:

> "I must have been about 15 when I became aware of my father as a man; I was then beginning to have beaux, but the affectionate idea, when I often sat on his lap, was that he was my best beau. I could not understand, a little later, why he was angry after I really fell in love with one of my young men and would spend a long time downstairs saying goodnight to him. At that time my father used to wear an old-fashioned nightshirt and walk around in it in the morning, and I was terrified—that's too strong a word—uneasy, that one day I might see his genitals. This never happened, but one morning he walked into my room while I was still in bed and kissed me and then he put his hand under the covers and ran it down my back. I suppose because I jumped, he then said something reassuring, 'You really are a woman now, aren't you?' I withdrew from him then, I think, and from that time his jealousy of my own life and my beaux began."

Fig. 7. "Devil": an Unconscious Symbol of the "Bad" Mother (Scribble).

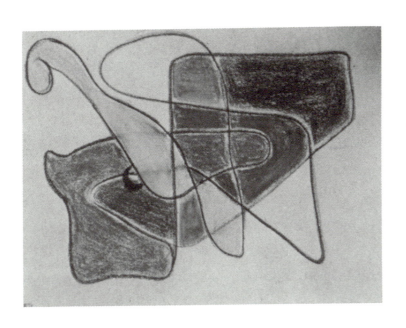

Fig. 6. Abstract Design (Scribble).

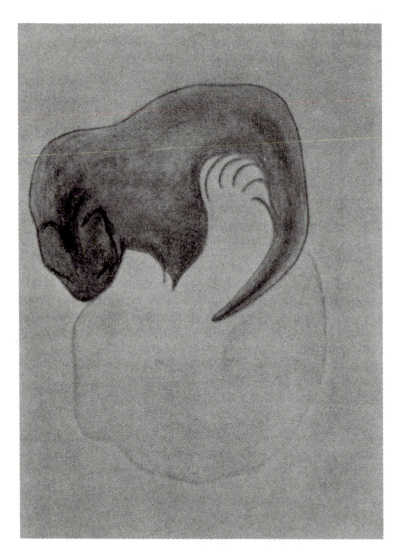

Fig. 8.   Double Fetal Form (Scribble).

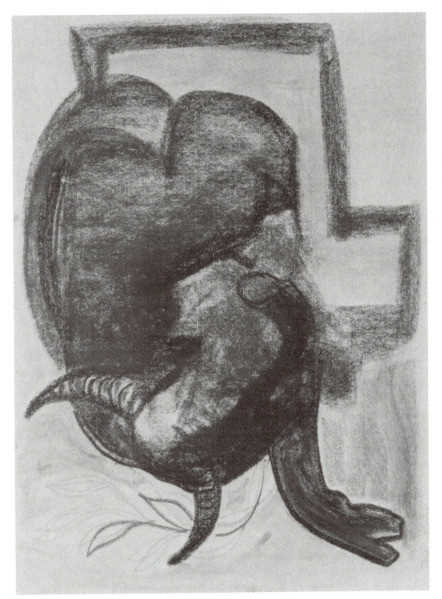

Fig. 9a. First Dream: the Bull Represents the Sexual Threat of the Father.

Second Dream: The Bull, as Father, Is Being Appeased with Silver Paper Packages by the Patient

Mrs. Felix said that the second bull picture (Fig. 9b) was also a dream; she explained that the oncoming bull was her father and that she, as the girl in the foreground, was attempting to appease the bull-father by throwing him silver paper packages as he came toward her. In the first of these two bull dreams she had expressed her fears of the sexual approaches of the father-bull. In the second bull dream she appeased his threatened sexual aggression. Other memories concerning her childhood relation to her father followed. She recalled that as a small child she had fallen into a puddle and soiled her underwear. She had lied to her father, saying she had fallen into the puddle in order to protect her brother, who had really pushed her in. The father, sensing her lie, punished her severely by refusing to speak to her for a week. Such severity, she recalled, had caused her to feel abandoned and deserted by her father. From that time, she said that she had experienced similar feelings of panic whenever the lover left her for a business trip or the husband threatened to break up their marriage.

The Release of Rage and Aggression in Pictures

The patient released her buried rage and aggression for the first time in a series of pictures in the sixth month of therapy. In a picture of herself in tears (not shown) she pointed to a jagged orange line and said, "I thought of that jagged line as my anger expressed in the shape of teeth." Following this design she made another, also derived from a scribble.

Mouth with Teeth and Tongue: as Symbol of Oral Regression (Scribble)

Two days after the rage design the patient projected this design with teeth (Fig. 10). "I knew that I was going to draw the teeth before I started," she said. "Then the tongue suggested itself, especially the quality of softness and helplessness before the devouring teeth. Then came the surrounding mouth, large and devouring, sucking everything into itself." It shows a typical passive and clinging response of the ulcer patient. She had previously attributed several of her oral designs to the devouring and overwhelming mother. Here Mrs. Felix's expression of helplessness repeats her frequently expressed victim psychology in the softness and helplessness of the tongue. She also related this picture to her feelings "when lying in bed with ulcer pain."

A Puppy Dog with a Bone: Threatened by the Claw-like Hand of the Mother (Elaborated from a doodle)

In the sixth month of therapy this large drawing of a dog with a bone (Fig. 11) was elaborated from an original small, pencil doodle, made by the patient while at a telephone. The patient said:

"This doodle recalls those other doodles that I made some months ago; then I drew M. N.'s face as the mother's, with me as a baby in her arms; I was reaching with my hand toward her breast. Remember how in the

Fig. 9b. Second Dream: The Bull, as Father, Is being Appeased with Silver Paper Packages by the Patient.

second of these mother-baby doodles I had unconsciously moved the hand of the baby so that it showed the baby reaching for the breast, but being denied it by the mother (Fig. 5b). In this dog picture, though, it's the black hand of the mother above the puppy that is the prohibiting agent. . . . This dog picture, with the bone and the clutching hand, seems to tie up with my preceding teeth and mouth pictures. Here is the helpless puppy with head bent down. Does this, I wondered, all go back to the time of my weaning? My mother said that she weaned me late and that I would 'follow her around like a little puppy dog.' I didn't recognize the full significance of this picture until after I wrote this down. Then I burst out laughing when I told all this to M. N."

Two Puppy Doodles

In the sixth month of therapy, in two successive weeks, two small doodles of puppy dogs were drawn by Mrs. Felix (Figs. 12a and 12b). The second doodle (Fig. 12b) shows a puppy exposing its teeth aggressively. The patient was most reluctant to show this second drawing, protesting, while withholding it, that it was unimportant. Finally, she admitted that she was both puzzled and disturbed by it. "I knew that the sucking mouth and the aggressive teeth seemed to contradict each other." Both of these puppy doodles clearly relate to the patient's longing to be loved and nursed by the protective mother. Such feelings had already been experienced in other typical oral regressive images of sucking and biting. They express the wish of the orally dependent patient to return to the breast. In the images of puppy teeth attacking a bone, Mrs. Felix expressed the release of her suppressed anger against the "bad" mother who had refused to continue nursing her.

Conflicts of the Patient

In the seventh month of therapy Mrs. Felix was able to realize for the first time that the flare-up of her ulcer pains occurred during emotional conflicts with her husband. She had observed the husband's particular interest in a young boy who visited them, and how her husband preferred this boy to his own son. She admitted that she had been trying to suppress the frightening implications that her husband's intimacy with this boy might imply that her husband was really a homosexual. If this were true, she recognized that she would have to break up her marriage. At the thought of permanent separation from her husband she became "panicky," for she was as yet unready to stand on her own feet. Although it would be several years before the patient would be able to admit the reality of her husband's inversion, she became gradually able, when she became anxious, to avoid escaping into ulcer symptoms as in the past. Now she began to be able to express her resistance to dealing with her anxieties by making pictures about them instead of going into a panic or developing ulcer symptoms.

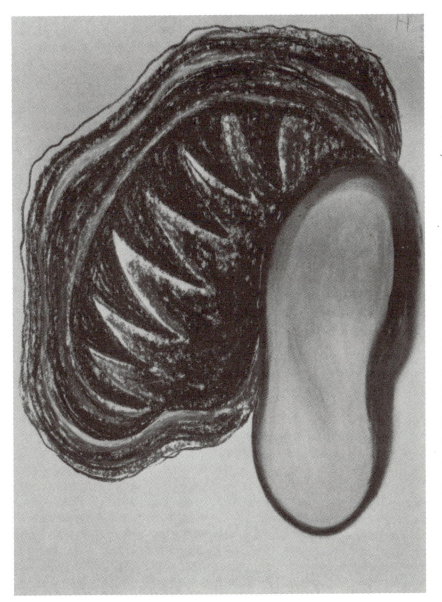

Fig. 10. Mouth with Teeth and Tongue: as Symbol of Oral Regression (Scribble).

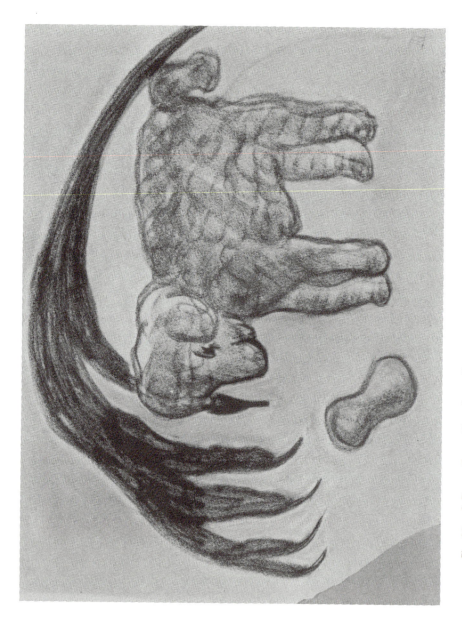

Fig. 11. A Puppy Dog with a Bone: Threatened by the Claw-like Hand of the Mother (Elaborated from a doodle).

Fig. 12a.

Two Puppy Doodles.

Fig. 12b.

The Mother Wolf and the Suckling Child (Begun as a scribble)

The head of the wolf in this picture (Fig. 13) was derived from a scribble. Some of the original, unused lines remain in evidence, but after drawing the wolf's head with its long jaw and sharp teeth the patient complained that there was no room left on the paper to complete the animal. It was suggested that another sheet of paper could be added. Mrs. Felix followed this suggestion and on the second sheet of paper drew quickly the wolf's three teats; but it is evident that these are drawn in the shape of human breasts and not animal teats— again an image of the patient's oral dependency on the mother. Beneath the teats she then drew the outline of a small child reaching for the breast. While making it, she commented, "There's only room here for one baby. There's no room for a second baby. I meant to have Romulus and Remus." As she said this she smiled, recognizing that she had expressed her unconscious impulse to keep her own baby brother away from the mother. "No competition here," she said. "There's no room here for another child; not even for feet or the threat of hands pushing away."

Recalling her previous puppy doodles, the patient said, "This mouth of the wolf is not a sucking mouth. Is one punished for trying to suck?" Asked to answer her own question, she said, "I felt the child in this picture recognized

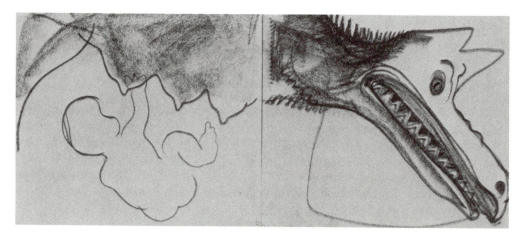

Fig. 13. The Mother Wolf and the Suckling Child (Begun as a scribble).

aggression in itself and the teeth here in the mother wolf are the destructive agent. It is in our vocabulary 'to be sucked in,' meaning to be destroyed. Even in this drawing, I can't make the child actually sucking the breast. I've never done it. As I drew, I realized that I got the child too far away from the mother wolf. In mythology the fascinating symbol has the child nursed by the wolf. The wolf is here the terrifying mother, that nurses but is frightening to the child. It seems to be a pattern. This wolf is the mother who wants to devour her children, perhaps."

"In what way did your mother want to devour you?" she was asked. "She wanted to make me dependent," said Mrs. Felix. "She was never so happy as I grew older as when I got sick and had to stay in bed a few days."

Recollections of the Family

"Why, when I draw pictures of family life is it always three, my mother, father and me? My brother isn't there. I haven't any feeling of rivalry. And yet, when I recently told my father that I thought my brother might have had a bad start in life by my being the favorite in the family, my father surprised me by saying that my brother was always my mother's favorite." Mrs. Felix said she then remembered that the mother had once told her, when she was fifteen, of how, when she was pregnant with her, she had tried to get rid of her by jumping up and down.

Recall of the Glamorous Mother and Cousin Who Made Her Feel Inferior

She again spoke of the beauty and charm of the mother and the cousin who lived in the household. "This cousin was glamorous but stupid. She had red hair like my mother. My father had puritanical disapproval of my mother's family. My father said my hair looked neat and sensible. It was straight and dark. My mother wanted it curly. She and my cousin took my beaux away from me and I had to do with second best. I never looked as pretty as my cousin. I felt awkward. I was the talented member of the family in contrast to my mother and cousin who were glamorous. As I got older I made capital of it."

Green Skull and Predatory Hands: an Unconscious Death Wish against the Father

This picture (Fig. 14) and the next one were painted in the eleventh month of therapy, after the summer holidays. They turned out to be unconscious projections of the patient's long repressed hostility and resentment against her parents. Both pictures were made at home. Since she had great difficulty in understanding the significance of these two designs, she was asked to describe the order in which she had drawn their various parts. About this Green Skull picture she said, "I made the green mass first. It suggested a skull to me, so I strengthened it to get a more primitive and brutal look." The brown around the skull she called "the shit color, because it represents rage on the childish level. Then came the predatory hands." She then referred back to the threatening hands of the mother in the large puppy painting from a doodle. "But unlike the puppy picture," she said, "this drawing is definitely tied to my father,

72 DYNAMICALLY ORIENTED ART THERAPY

and not to my mother. . . . The red profile at the left is most important. . . . It began as a stern god-like face; I thought a father-god, but it changed and represented Minerva."

She then developed the idea that she, like Minerva who sprang full-born from Jupiter's head, was the product of her father's rationalist, nineteenth century point of view. "In this way," she explained, "I got split off from my own base. This picture as a whole seems to mark the beginning of adolescence. With that orange color I blotted out my own creativity, to become the intellectual product of my father. This shows what my father did to my feminine and creative side. He hated my painting, but I went on loving him. I didn't see that I was giving up my real self. I guess this skull . . ." she hesitated. "Why it's a death wish against my father! I didn't see it before! I refused then to admit that my father was wrong because I had to have this hero worship about him; and still there was the need to have my own creativity. There was this struggle inside of me against giving up my creativity in art. I had the intellectual companionship of my father and would never let my negative feelings against my cousin come out for taking my beaux away from me."

"Now the Cat is out of the Bag"

Mrs. Felix said, "This second picture (Fig. 15) isn't as important as the Green Skull picture; it's not so deep. It's a play on words; it says, 'Now the cat is out of the bag.' But the first picture is the real material."

In order to overcome the patient's evident resistance to associating freely to this second cat design, she was asked to explain the steps in its creation. Her response revealed the profound symbolic significance of this second picture.

"I began," she said, "with the olive green diagonal line. The lighter green, seen as a free wiggle, suggested a cat, and then I made its claws. Here comes the brown again. This animal is raking up the muck of the past. Why bother with it? A feeling of disgust. At the end, I put in that bleeding mouse, there (lower left corner). Then I put in that hand with a finger pointing back to that muck, which I don't like. I wonder whether it's your stern finger telling me to go back this way. The bleeding mouse, I think, represents myself as a victim. . . . I had it bleeding at both ends, blood from the mouth and rectum. Shit. The ulcer stands for rage—the bleeding, intestinal business."

Mrs. Felix Then Reviewed the Significance of Both These Pictures as Referring to Her Father and Mother

"In the previous picture of the green skull I said, 'I hate my father,' I drew the skull but couldn't, while creating it, admit the death wish. It was only after you asked me to explan how I had painted it that I dared look again at this skull image and admit this long repressed wish against my father.

"You said last time I should try to catch the mood I felt and not draw consciously. I recognized the feeling in the Skull picture against my father, as expressed in a vomit green. That green is the color of a corpse; it stands

Fig. 14.   Green Skull and Predatory Hands: an Unconscious Death Wish against the
Father. Color plate on page xi.

Fig. 15.   "Now the Cat is out of the Bag." Color plate on page xi.

for putrefaction. But the green I've used in the cat picture suggests my mother more than my father. The cat is feminine to me. The hands of the cat struggle with the father for the possession of the mouse. And it's the mother cat who brings in the dead mice. The cat we have at home is a long green-eyed hunter. She's ferocious. It's my daughter's cat and I would love to get rid of it."

The patient was utterly surprised when it was pointed out to her how she had unconsciously identified the daughter's cat with her feelings about her own mother, who had been destructive to her life. She had identified herself with the bleeding mouse associated with the blood-red ulcer symbol, and now she understood that the cat stood for her mother as killing her, the mouse.

The Patient's Disturbance over Her Expressed Hostility to Both Her Parents

In reviewing what her free associations had uncovered in relation to these two pictures, the patient was reminded that her resistance about speaking of the Cat picture had been even stronger than it was about the Skull design. She was also reminded that while she called the second picture "Now The Cat Is out of the Bag," the cat was actually only *half* out, and that there was probably a great deal more for her still to discover about this cat. The patient laughed in recognition of the truth of this comment.

Since Mrs. Felix was deeply troubled by the extent of her hostility against her parents, as shown in these two pictures, it was necessary to give her considerable supportive aid. She was reminded that these designs were released as the consequence of a year of therapy in which she had been able gradually to uncover very deep material concerning her earlier relationship to both her parents. She was asked to remember that only by disentangling what she now recognized as genuine and positive aspects of her relation to both her parents could she begin to establish herself firmly within her present life situation. Now that the patient was beginning to understand the way in which the neurotic needs of both her parents had been projected onto her during her childhood and adolescence, she was assured that she was now strong enough to no longer need to escape from either parents or husband by reverting to her previously recurrent ulcer symptoms.

"Green Elephant and Grey Shark, Combined with Black Square of Depression and Orange Core of Hope" (Scribble)

This design (Fig. 16) was made by Mrs. Felix a week after the Skull and Cat pictures, which had dealt with her disturbed relation to her parents. The patient explained that this Elephant picture was an attempt to bring together the masculine and feminine aspects of her nature. She called it "Green Elephant and Grey Shark." In the lower left-hand corner, she said, was an elephant with his trunk pointing upward, its color "benign." This other animal, she said, "looks like a grey shark upside down. The black center square expresses depression— my suffering. The red over the black expresses my creativity. The center orange triangular shape, that's the core of hope."

"See," Mrs. Felix continued, "there are no teeth in the elephant's mouth, it's sucking and toothless. The trunk is masculine and the mouth is feminine. The grey shark with scales is masculine, voracious and toothed." Here again she had emphasized her concern about both sucking and biting.

"This picture with the elongated elephant's trunk," she explained, "reminds me of my earlier dream about my mother's genitals, in which I painted a penis symbol emerging from her face. It was that oil portrait of my mother (Fig 4). I remember that when I had that vivid dream about my mother's genitals being in her face, I thought then, 'Who would want to make love to a woman like that?'"

Mouth with Tongue

The patient had much hesitation in showing this small doodle (Fig. 17) to the therapist. She had buried it in her purse. When she finally brought it forth reluctantly, she said, "It's awful; it tells the whole story." When asked to explain what she meant, she began by saying that she had drawn it in between the time she had been with her lover and this appointment with the therapist. She understood, she said, the meaning of the huge mouth and its large tongue. In this doodle, she explained, "the tongue is also a penis." As she said this she again referred to the dream about her mother's genitals with penis attached (Fig. 4), an image that she had already referred to several times.

Fig. 16. "Green Elephant and Grey Shark, Combined with Black Square of Depression and Orange Core of Hope" (Scribble).

When the therapist observed that the doodle suggested the act of fellatio, the patient became embarrassed because she knew that this was what she had drawn. She then admitted having practiced fellatio with the lover, but had not informed the therapist because she feared that such action might be misunderstood. She then emphasized that because of her deep and warm relation with her lover, all variations in sexual intimacy became possible.

The lover's imminent departure on a business trip again threw her into a panic. She said that she had tried, as before, to end the relation but found herself unable to do so. She was reminded that her present panic went back to that first one in her childhood which occurred with her father's refusal to speak to her for a week.

"A Green Frog-like Creature Representing Myself: an Expression of Sexual Confusion in Childhood"

One of her childhood memories about sex the patient remembered as "A Green Frog-like Creature Representing Myself." This picture (Fig. 18), she said, recalled a childhood memory of the two different ways she had been taught

Fig. 17.   Mouth with Tongue.

to wipe herself on the toilet: her aunt had taught her to wipe herself from the front, and the mother from behind. These recollections she felt related to aspects of sexuality. "It must," she said, "have had something to do with masturbation. The pink mass in the picture reminded me of my mother's red hair. Again she was the prohibiting agent who forbade me to wipe myself from the front when on the toilet. Wouldn't you say this lower part of the creature looked like a behind? When I first drew it, I thought it was a female front view, but next day it looked more like a behind view. It seems to me that this picture answers the knowledge and the not knowing about sex. There is complete confusion in this picture!"

Fig. 18. "A Green Frog-like Creature Representing Myself: an Expression of Sexual Confusion in Childhood."

"Myself Running Away" (Scribble)

The patient had avoided seeing the therapist for a month. She brought with her this picture of "Myself, Running Away" (Fig. 19), explaining that she made it from a scribble after telephoning for an appointment. "It says," she continued, "being on the defensive with the therapist for having avoided an appointment for so long." Laughing self-consciously, she commented, "It's gay and rather amusing." She then told how before her trip to New York she had made this picture. "I began with a brown scribble. A running figure emerged;

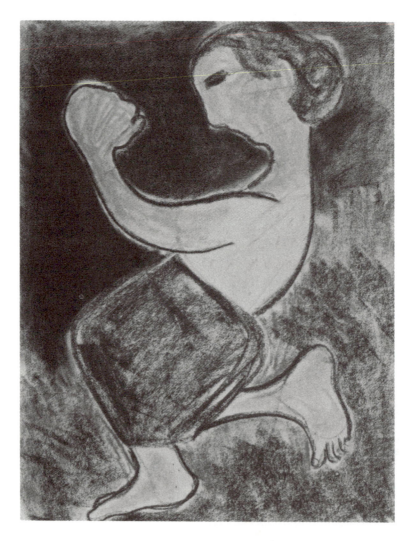

Fig. 19. "Myself Running Away" (Scribble).

a defined head, a body position which at first seemed fighting, but then the feet turned out to be running away. The skirt suggested binding. Perhaps a feminine handicap? The black background stands for an unknown destination. The yellow suggests light." Mrs. Felix was surprised, she said, to discover how, when she had finished this picture, it had turned into one of herself running away. Three months before she had also drawn a picture of herself as a child, but in that one she was running away from the sexual threat of a strange man.

Mrs. Felix explained her long postponement about making an appointment as due to her sudden decision to sue for divorce. When she had announced her plan, her husband, to her surprise, refused as in the past to accept her proposal for divorce and stated that he would obstruct her action. She still refused to face the reason that her husband found the status quo of their marriage quite convenient. Angered by his attitude, she had tried to shock his puritanism by shouting "bull shit" at him. She had used this term also in her Bull dream about the father.

Mrs. Felix said she also tried to shock her husband's sexual repressions by speaking frankly to her children about sex in his presence. She then recalled what she still tried to regard as his prudishness when she remembered that he had objected to her being naked on their wedding night, nor had he exposed his own nudity to her. During her years of marriage she had passively accepted this attitude of her husband.

When Mrs. Felix had been shown how unrealistic and ambivalent her attitude to her husband had been, it was gradually possible to help her to face the way that she had always rationalized her own motives for seeking a divorce. She was reminded of how often she had impulsively told her husband that she must have a divorce, but had then panicked at her inability to envisage life without depending on the father-figure of her husband.

"The Patient as a Pleading Child behind Her Parents" (Doodle)

A small doodle of "The Patient as a Pleading Child behind her Parents" (Fig. 20) was also shown to the therapist at this time. It again revealed the continuing, unconscious release of the patient's oral dependence on the authority of both parental figures.

Hermaphrodite Form: Representing Masculine and Feminine Aspects of the Patient (Doodle)

In this doodle drawing of a Hermaphrodite Form: Representing Masculine and Feminine Aspects of the Patient (Fig. 21), Mrs. Felix had released unconscious feelings which embarrassed her greatly. She therefore withheld the picture until the end of the session.

She made this doodle while flying to New York for her art therapy session and was both surprised and disturbed at what she had created. She knew, she said, that the two heads which she had drawn were two aspects of herself, combined in one body. The head of the man with the large aggressive penis, she told the therapist, represented her more aggressive self, and the female head represented, she thought, a combination of her mother and herself. The feminine looking figure in the sitting position suggested evacuation to her. This led the patient to recall her aggressive self-assertion in relation to her repeated use of the term "bull shit." She then explained that she had added the large heart which seemed to stand for a body, and after that she had drawn the tiny symbolic spine, which showed transparently through the heart.

"A Doodle, Begun as a Woman, Turns into a Man"

"Although this doodle (Fig. 22) started as a woman," said Mrs. Felix, "it turned into a man." She made this doodle five months after the previous one. It too deals with the male-female aspects of personality. The patient had interpreted her previous doodle as relating to her aggressive-dependent self, but this one she associated with her husband. "Although I started this as a woman, I made it something like a man. The female head," she said, "seems attached to a breast. The large phallus," she continued, "which is drawn in the center of the picture, I wanted to remove. But if I do, I said to myself, I'm not being honest." She then told the therapist, "This doodle reminds me of my husband, who has both masculine and feminine features." Since this hint of her husband's possible inversion frightened her again, she then recalled a woman friend's accusations that she had castrated her husband by her aggressive behavior. "Suppose," she said, "I'm such a castrating female. Such a thought gives me a feeling of being trapped. If it's true, I'm lost. It gives me a feeling of helplessness on the childish level."

Fig. 20.   "The Patient as a Pleading Child behind Her Parents" (Doodle).

Here again, Mrs. Felix returned to her longing for dependence on her husband. She now referred to a feeling of guilt about her aggressive behavior in order to avoid recognizing that her husband's passivity toward her was related to his inversion. Self pity followed when she asked melodramatically, "Why, if I couldn't be a glamour girl, couldn't I free the creative thing and be more successful in my art?"

Male Figure Symbolizing the Ambivalence of the Patient (Doodle)

Here is another doodle (Fig. 23) drawn by Mrs. Felix in the same month as the two previous ones. She said that she drew it on the back of an envelope while telephoning. You can see where one side of a triangular envelope flap becomes the slant of the chain that the man is pulling. Mrs. Felix recognized that this male figure, drawing on the chain in order to raise the cover from the ground, was a symbol of her aggressive self. She also noted that the man was at the same moment pressing his foot against this cover in order to prevent it from revealing what lay beneath. She was aware as soon as she had drawn it, she said, that her unconscious had projected a true picture of the way she felt, for in this doodle she saw that her foot was trying to push back her conflicts

Fig. 21. Hermaphrodite Form: Representing Masculine and Feminine Aspects of the Patient (Doodle).

Fig. 22. "A Doodle, Begun as a Woman, Turns into a Man."

Fig. 23. Male Figure Symbolizing the Ambivalence of the Patient (Doodle).

out of sight while her hands were pulling at her chain in order to uncover what lay concealed underground. At this point in therapy, the patient was able to recognize and admit that what she had expressed in this doodle was her desire to avoid examining her repressed conflicts. Understanding the symbolism of this doodle, she was now able to laugh at the contradictory behavior that it expressed.

Another Mother Portrait: Projection of the Patient's Unconscious Hostility against the Mother

This caricature of the mother (Fig. 24), painted in the seventh month of therapy on flimsy newsprint paper, was made three weeks before Mrs. Felix was willing to show it to the therapist. The patient admitted that she had been terribly disturbed by this painting, and she felt ashamed and guilty at having created such a caricature of her mother. "When I began this painting," she said, "it started as a classical head with simplified eyes and the nose of a man. Then I added lots of brown curls on top of the head. Then the head took on the familiar characteristics of other faces that I've done of my mother. Interesting additions were the masculine-feminine confusion in the design. That reminds

Fig. 24. Another Mother Portrait: Projection of the Patient's Unconscious Hostility against the Mother. Color plate on page x.

me that mother always said that she gave up a musical career for having babies. My mother's conflict over her own feminine role may have caused me to draw her this way. As I recognized my mother's face in the picture, I went over the brown curls and made them red. I made her eyes green, an unconscious choice, as her eyes were really brown." The green of the eyes was then interpreted by the patient as jealousy; she said that she had heard her mother use the words "green-eyed monster" to express jealousy. Then Mrs. Felix added, "I again changed the color of the hair, adding yellow to make its red-gold like my young cousin's. Both my mother and grandmother wore such high collars as I painted in this portrait. I think I put my mother in a straitjacket with this high collar. Finally, I added rouge to her cheeks to purposely cheapen the woman." But the patient had, by this time, gained sufficient insight through her therapy to comment, "I see now this isn't really a portrait of my mother but a picture of one of my attitudes toward my mother."

Mrs. Felix frightened again by the degree of hostility that she had released against her mother in this portrait, suspended regular art therapy sessions during the summer months and also during much of the next two years. She maintained, however, an intermittent contact with the therapist. At such times she would report on the progress of her hospital work and the state of her family problems. During the following winter, she decided to join an art therapy seminar offered by the therapist to art educators. She then began therapy sessions again, but the realization at this time that her mother's worldly and economic ambitions, which she despised, had originally influenced her choice of husbands in both her marriages was such a shock to her that she did not want to deal as yet with its implications. Nor was Mrs. Felix as yet able to face the implications of her husband's inversion. Only four years later, with irrefutable proof of her husband's homosexuality, did she get her divorce. She was then able to continue and complete her therapy sessions successfully.

II. IMAGES AND HALLUCINATIONS OF AN ALCOHOLIC PATIENT*

Art therapy, in its encouragement of visual projection into pictorial images, seems to offer a very suitable technique for the expression of visual hallucinations and images released by an alcoholic. How this approach was employed in the treatment of Miss Elton, a chronic alcoholic woman 41 years old, will be related to the pictures that she produced and to her own interpretation of their symbolic meaning. The patient's history, including her past and present life and recollections, will be presented in the order in which they were obtained from the patient, rather than in the usual case history method.

Miss Elton had originally been informed about the art therapy approach by a woman friend who was acquainted with the therapist. She became sufficiently interested in the possibilities to ask this friend to arrange an appointment with the art therapist. Before the first meeting occurred, the friend had informed the therapist about Miss Elton's history of chronic alcoholism.

When Miss Elton came to the introductory meeting with her friend, she was not drinking and gave the impression of being intelligent, sensitive and alert. She was eager to talk about herself and immediately mentioned some of her disturbing hallucinations. One of these, she said, appeared as an enormous cliff which overwhelmed her. The other recurrent image was a huge monster which always sapped her strength. In telling of these hallucinations, Miss Elton emphasized to the therapist that this was the first time that she had ever told anyone about these frightening experiences. Both the cliff image and the monster image played significant symbolic roles in many of the patient's pictures during the early art therapy sessions.

---

* Presented in brief at the meeting of the New York Medical Society on Alcoholism, April 20, 1955, at the Academy of Medicine, New York City. An exhibition of this alcoholic woman's pictures was shown at the Annual Meeting of the American Psychiatric Association, in Atlantic City, N. J., May 9-13, 1955.

After confiding these hallucinations to the therapist, Miss Elton showed her an oil painting which she had brought. She explained that in this picture she had tried to paint her experience with the cliff image. Miss Elton then told that when years ago she had shown this oil painting (which was quite amateurish) to a professional artist, he had laughed at it. This had so upset her that she had slashed away the cliff in the picture and had never tried to paint again.

When a brief explanation of the principles of the art therapy approach was offered to Miss Elton, she became much interested. The fact that the spontaneous creation of pictures could release repressed feelings more easily than words struck a responsive chord in Miss Elton, and she asked whether it would not be possible for her to begin art therapy sessions immediately.

Because of Miss Elton's known history of chronic alcoholism, a certain tentative approach had to be considered. She was therefore told that a few preliminary trial sessions would be needed in order to enable the therapist to judge whether this therapeutic approach would be suitable for her. She then agreed to undertake three trial sessions.

Preliminary Financial Arrangements

After Miss Elton had agreed to the preliminary trial sessions, she said that she would be able to pay the therapist on the basis of a new secretarial job she was about to get. A minimum fee was then suggested to which she agreed. Miss Elton was never to earn a living during the art therapy sessions. When the money was offered for this purpose by her older sister, she refused to pay the therapist for various specious reasons, which will later be explained as illustrative of the patient's ambivalent and frequently hostile attitude toward the therapist.

THREE PRELIMINARY TRIAL SESSIONS

During the first two sessions Miss Elton was so confused and produced so many chaotic pictures about her struggle with the monster in her room that it seemed unlikely that the sessions could continue. In the third session, however, important childhood memories, as well as aspects of her relation to both a previous therapist and the present therapist, were projected into significant pictures.

The First Session

Miss Elton was two hours late to her first evening appointment. She was apologetic and embarrassed and explained that her lateness was due to her great resistance to coming. Throughout this first session she spoke in a confused and often incoherent manner. She mumbled about the terror of the experiences she had been undergoing during the past few days, "fighting the monster" in her room.

After listening sympathetically to the patient's fragmentary and excited description of her hallucinations, she was offered a box of pastels and paper and asked whether she might care to draw her struggle with this monster. She first protested that she could not draw people, but when urged to try she sat down and began to make one of a series of seven chaotic drawings. She talked in jumbled incomprehensible phrases as she worked.

There were seven of these "monster" pictures drawn in green chalk, in quick succession. A picture of the first one is shown.

First Monster Drawing: the Patient's Struggle with the Monster

In this first picture (Fig. 25) Miss Elton drew her fight with what she called "a green, fat, slimy monster with many mouths that sucked my strength." During her garbled talk she significantly gave the monster the names of both her older brothers. (A number of her later pictures reveal how these brothers abused her when she was young.) As she drew this picture, the patient became increasingly excited while describing her efforts to battle this monster by "sitting it out in my room."

Six other hastily drawn pictures (not shown) continued to show the patient's struggle with this monster. Her explanations of what happened in these pictures were too jumbled to follow. Miss Elton's disturbed condition during this and the next session suggested possible psychosis. Her disassociated condition was, it turned out, due to an excessive use of Dexedrine, for the patient had substituted an addiction to Dexedrine to replace both alcohol and Antabuse.

At the end of an hour and a half, it became difficult to rouse Miss Elton from her trance-like state and make her realize that the art therapy session was over. The patient, before leaving, said that she would make more pictures before the next session. As she had no art materials of her own and could not afford to buy them, she was given a box of pastels and some paper to take home with her.

Miss Elton's many pictures of her continuing battle with the monster seem to be a visual confirmation of what Dr. Ruth Fox, the eminent authority on alcoholism, has written concerning the role of alcohol: "Alcohol can be looked on almost as an outside force against which the patient carries on an endless struggle."[1]

Second Session

During the second session the patient continued her struggle with the monster.

The Green Monster and the Huge Breast

The patient said that while drawing this second series of monster pictures she had no idea what they meant. This session took place nine days after the first session. Miss Elton brought in seven pictures which she had drawn at home. Her designs were still confused, showing monsters, crosses and several figures of herself in various positions, but they showed improvement over her first

---

[1] Fox, Ruth: "Psychotherapeutics of Alcoholism." *Specialized Techniques in Psychotherapy* (Eds. Gustav Bychowski and J. Louise Despert). New York, Basic Books, 1952, p. 243.

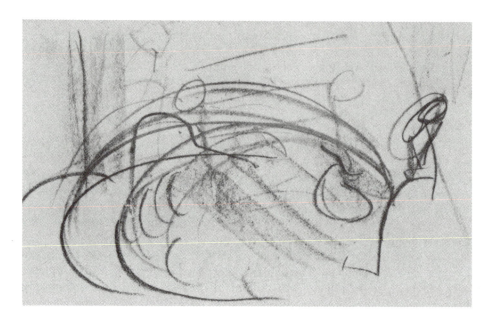

Fig. 25.   First Monster Drawing: the Patient's Struggle with the Monster.

Fig. 26.   The Green Monster and Huge Breast.

ones. She had now begun to use many of the colored pastels instead of the single green one of her first pictures. The large rounded shape of her monster was now more developed than in some of the pictures. In her drawing of The Green Monster and the Huge Breast (Fig. 26), the patient sits facing the more solidified form of the green monster, while a huge breast was drawn in front of it. This breast, Miss Elton said, reminded her of her mother who had been unable to nurse her. (More about this appeared in later pictures.)

Figure of the Patient with the Monster Chained Below

In the upper part of this picture (Fig. 27) Miss Elton sits in a chair with her bed placed opposite her. In the lower part of this design, below the level of her room, are two other forms. The rounded shape bound by a chain showed the same monster who, she said, was under control for the first time. The brightly colored form beside the monster represented, she said, her unconscious, which was now being freed.

Third Session

Recall of Childhood Memories

In a telephone talk between the second and third art therapy sessions, Miss Elton had excitedly told the therapist about some early childhood memories that had come back to her with some new pictures that she had just drawn. When she brought them to the therapist the next day, she was feeling happy about her achievement. These new designs showed an improved sense of organization and specific meaning. She was eager to explain their significance.

"Bright Colors in the Center of a Dark Picture: It's a Ray of Light and Hope Working with M.N."

This is what Miss Elton called her almost black design (Fig. 28) with its single streak of light. Here she had given pictorial expression to the beginning of her positive transference to the therapist, but as the patient's subsequent images showed, she was soon to express her typical ambivalence as an alcoholic patient in a number of hostile pictures about the therapist.

The words "Rockabye baby on the tree-top, when the wind blows the cradle will fall" were recited by the patient as associated with her second picture (not shown because it was too dark to photograph). Her design had, according to her own description, two separate parts. The upper section showed a rounded black shape containing a bright red curved form. This, Miss Elton explained, represented the face of her colored mammy, who had cared for her in the South until she was three years old. The "Rockabye Baby" title which she had given this picture was associated to the songs that her mammy used to sing her. Miss Elton then recalled that her mother had never nursed her but had sent her beloved mammy away when the patient was three years old. She also remembered her mother saying that her milk had been "poison" to the patient, and had never nursed her. In the previous therapy session, the patient had drawn a huge breast (Fig. 26) which probably related to the patient's sense

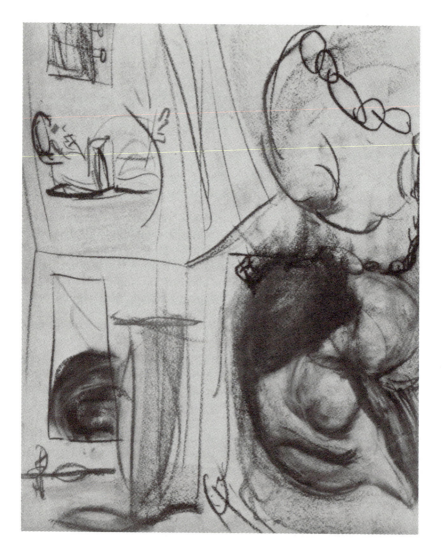

Fig. 27.   Figure of the Patient with the Monster Chained below.

of oral deprivation, which is so frequent in alcoholics. This exaggeratedly large breast drawing may have also been related to Miss Elton's concern about her mother's death from breast cancer.

In the lower part of this same picture the patient has drawn a small bush with orange blossoms. Miss Elton explained that the orange flowers were poison because they were the color of Dexedrine. She then referred, for the first time, to her own anxiety about her dependence on Dexedrine. A small orange figure reclines at the bottom of this picture on the magenta couch. The symbolism of these two combined colors is of special significance, because the magenta color of the couch appears later in several pictures as being the mother's particular color. Therefore, the orange Dexedrine color figure of the patient lying upon the magenta couch, which used the mother's own color, suggests an effort on the part of the patient to regain contact with her real mother. In the sixth picture of this session, "The Dead Mother and the Black Coffin" (Fig. 30), the mother is robed in a magenta gown that the patient remembered seeing her wear. And again, when Miss Elton drew a picture of a visit to her mother in an insane asylum, she drew her in a magenta gown.

"I am Clinging to the Cliff While the Sun Looks Down at Me with a Mocking Smile."

This is a strangely poignant picture (Fig. 29) in which the patient has pictured herself as a small orange figure (the Dexedrine color) clinging, as she said, "against a dark and threatening cliff." (Again there is the recurrent image of the cliff.) High up, in the center of the picture, is the huge face of the sun which, she said, "looks down at me with a mocking smile." The sun is offering her in this picture a cord to rescue her, but it fails to do so because it is too short to reach down to her at the base of the cliff. But on the other side of the chasm, the patient emphasizes that there is another height "of a clear mountainous form"; this, she says, stands for the hope which she feels about the new work in art therapy. After making this picture, Miss Elton wrote in her diary that when she made the picture she had the feeling of "being engulfed." "I was unable," she wrote, "to climb to Dr. G's side or mine. I clung to my cliff blindly, knowing only: Faith is now."

In this picture, the patient had expressed hostility to Dr. G., the previous therapist, for failing to save her from herself.

The Dead Mother and the Black Coffin

In the forefront of this picture (Fig. 30) lies a figure in a magenta gown, and behind it, slightly to the right, is seen what the patient called "a black coffin." In the distance are several small orange figures. When Miss Elton showed this picture to the therapist, she said, "At first I wondered whether the black coffin was mine. But then I saw that the dead figure wore the magenta tea gown that my mother wore when I was a child." The small orange (Dexedrine color) figures were, the patient said, herself.

Fig. 28. "Bright Colors in the Center of a Dark Picture: It's a Ray of Light and Hope Working with M.N." Color plate on page xii.

Fig. 29. "I Am Clinging to the Cliff While the Sun Looks Down at Me with a Mocking Smile." Color plate on page xii.

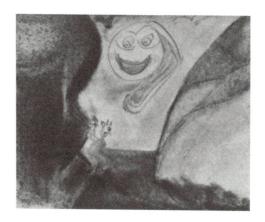

Fig. 30. The Dead Mother and the Black Coffin. Color plate on page xii.

The Patient's Apostrophe to the Dead Mother

In her diary Miss Elton wrote a significant apostrophe to her dead mother.

"Women must be beautiful and mysterious. (Women must have clear brows and clouded eyes?) Woman can be what she will behind the proud enigma of her beauty. (Beautiful and mysterious . . . and dead?)

"Erect, imperious in your mauve crepe de chine tea gown you stood beside the grand piano and wished for fifty slaves. I hated you with the purity of childhood because when I was nine I hated slavery. I remembered how you'd tossed your head and thought that I was cute when I had suddenly been hurt because I was five years old and didn't know whether my Irish Terrier was white or colored. I learned a lot from the way you enjoyed and ignored my question as cute and inconsequential.

"Mother! Mother! Lying there dead with your bland brow! Lying there in that same mauve tea gown; why are you out of your coffin all these years? See! I've made it to fit you—not me! I am frightened, mother, by the deadliness contained within your corpse beside the black box.

"Last night for the thousandth night I dreamed I kept your death watch like a friend and daughter should. . . .

"Mother, Sweet? Do you know in death what you never knew in life? What things I must unlearn.

"My blood is pale mauve to brighten your tea gown. I hate you, mother. My pale mauve heart is incapable of love.

"Mother."

The Patient Kneels Beside an Explosion: and as a Child Is Being Pinched in the Stomach by Her Brother

In this picture (Fig. 31) several events in the patient's history are shown. The large central figure, she said, was herself kneeling while an explosion, with objects flying about, surrounds her. "This explosion," she explained, "stands for the state of anxiety I'm in, for fear that the art therapy sessions won't go on after today." (These comments about her picture were made before she had been informed that she had qualified so as to continue the art therapy sessions.) "My anxiety," she said, "is reinforced by the large threatening arm I drew behind my own kneeling figure." On the right upper part of this picture, Miss Elton has drawn a lovely multicolored circular form, but she did not explain its meaning. Such an image frequently relates to the symbolic unification of self. This rounded form is drawn beside a landscape on the upper part of the design. The patient described the landscape of purple hills and trees placed within an arch as a "lover's paradise." This scene, she explained, "stood for hope." In this comment she was referring to her hope that the art therapy sessions would be continued.

The second part of the picture relates to a small upright form behind her own kneeling figure. This, Miss Elton said, represents herself as a small child, with red tears falling from her eyes. The large hand which was pinching her belonged, she explained, to her older brother. This was the first picture drawn

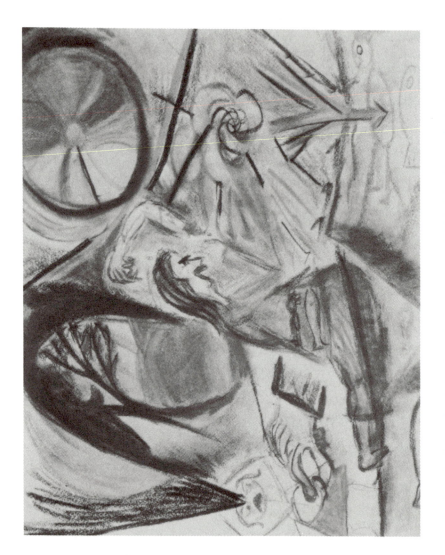

Fig. 31. The Patient Kneels Beside an Explosion: and as Child is Being Pinched in the Stomach by Her Brother.

by the patient of her older brother's sadistic treatment of her as a child. Many others appeared later.

Extracts from the Patient's Diary Written before the Art Therapy Sessions

At the second session Miss Elton had offered to show the therapist what she had written in her diary about "the unconscious." These notes were dated a month before the art sessions began and were evidently written while she was still seeing the previous therapist. Her writing is filled with chaotic sentences and fragmented thoughts that recall her condition during the first art therapy session. These notes show deep depression, speak much about death, and refer to a recurrent impulse toward self-destruction. The patient also speaks of her feelings of guilt, self-abuse and self-pity. There is protest also against the routine requirements of a secretarial job. These diary notes reveal a typical alcoholic personality pattern.

Consultation with Previous Therapist Following Three Trial Art Therapy Sessions

After the trial sessions, a consultation was held with Dr. G., the therapist who had treated Miss Elton both medically and psychiatrically for several years. He was impressed with this therapist's report on the patient's positive and revealing response in the three preliminary art sessions, and he expressed to both the therapist and the patient his willingness to support this new therapeutic approach. It was arranged that the patient would continue to see her previous therapist at intervals because of her deep fear of rejection. The present therapist also arranged to keep in touch with this psychiatrist and keep him informed about the development of Miss Elton in her art therapy sessions. This arrangement enabled the psychiatrist to keep a check on the patient's physical and emotional condition and would also make it possible for him to continue his reports about Miss Elton's condition to her sister, who, living at a distance, had continued to finance the patient's medical care and support.

CLINICAL HISTORY

This brief report on Miss Elton's family history is derived from several sources. Some of the information was obtained from the patient in the course of therapy, and additional facts came from her former therapist as well as the woman friend who had introduced her to the present therapist.

Miss Elton was the youngest of five children. She had two sisters and two brothers; the sisters were six and fifteen years older than the patient, and the two brothers were fourteen and ten years older.

Miss Elton was born in Kentucky, where her father, a wealthy Latin-American industrialist, had settled. There he married the patient's mother, who belonged to an old Southern family. There are a number of disturbing aspects to the patient's early family life that must have influenced the development of her chronic alcoholism. She had been deeply attached to her father, who, because of business reverses, committed suicide when the patient was fifteen. The extent of her strong identification with her father was revealed when she had pantomimed her own suicide at school to her friends. In a number of her pictures and comments the patient also expressed her hostility against her father for killing himself.

The Following Notes by the Patient May Have Been Part of Her Proposed Autobiography:

"Over the years my unconsciousness has seen again and again the same small death I now propose. It strokes the beasts of dread and hopelessness. In a year or less they'll nip at me until I nearly choke from running. I'll probably call them Sterile and Waste or some other names that describe unlove again.

"My unconscious states full awareness that I'm stretching debt far into the future—punishing myself for frustration and inability to formulate a valid escape to life. It professes full contact with the reality that each day I burn another outpost of the independence and freedom to move made possible by money. It seems to remember what no money was— and need—and to know I'm courting them. It reacts with distaste but not alarm. . . . My unconscious remembers when this same death looked on the joy of creation sparkling with the love and care that gave meaning to its young achievements. My unconscious remembers death's words of banishment: 'You're not genius. You're third rate and silly. Your attitude is wrong for the atmosphere I plan. I'm in charge; I say that here there is no longer time nor space nor work nor food for you. Nor any acknowledgment by memory that you ever belonged here or were anything but silly.'

"My unconscious then received no bread nor water for the next 16 years. Nor any acknowledgment by memory that it once belonged or was ever more than silly. . . . My unconscious had experienced pain and withering hunger. Memory acknowledged *them*. But my unconscious had discovered how fully its creativeness belonged. Sixteen years offered themselves with love. . . . Now death is back. It seems again he might take charge. My unconscious has withdrawn all desire within its dark inner hideness not to be misused again. Joy and hope are withdrawn and protected too; and silliness. All energy is withdrawn as well except 15 per cent for token functioning. . . . My unconscious states it never need play dead again. It is aware it may die in this present struggle. This reality finds itself acknowledged by regret without alarm or compromise.

"Should this phoney death win out, it says we'll laugh and thieve and work and hide, briefly."

Although the patient told the therapist, "I have forgiven my father," she was surprised to discover in the course of the art therapy sessions how intensely she still resented her father's self-destructive action.

The mother was known to have been an alcoholic long before the father's death. As her condition grew worse, she became psychotic as well. She was institutionalized at various times. The patient has described how, following the father's suicide, the mother had turned a pistol on her and threatened to kill her when Miss Elton tried to withhold alcohol from her at the doctor's orders. The patient's relation to the mother was always intensely ambivalent and much of the material produced in the art therapy sessions illustrate this conflict between her love and hate of the mother. In the latter part of the mother's life, the patient lived with the mother after removing her from an institution. The mother died some years later of cancer. The patient, who was unable to endure looking after the mother during this final illness, continued during therapy sessions to express guilt about her inability to face caring for her dying mother.

The oldest sister married well and moved to a distant city when the patient was quite young. She was the only individual in the family who, from available reports, remained quite stable. She has stood by the patient and continued to help her financially throughout her difficulties. More about this sister, and the patient's ambivalent attitude toward her, developed during the therapy sessions and is reported later.

The second sister also married and left the South. She seems to have played no significant role in the patient's life. Considerable information concerning the patient's relation to the two brothers was obtained from her during the therapy sessions.

Miss Elton stated that after the father's death the older brother, sixteen years her senior, was given control of the family finances. She insisted that this brother cheated her out of her share of the family estate; she also insisted that he had the mother institutionalized and kept incarcerated when she had recovered, as a means of obtaining her income for himself. The older brother never married. The second brother, however, did marry, but was later divorced. Both brothers drank heavily and it is possible that they too were alcoholics. In the first art therapy sessions it became evident that the patient was deeply critical and resentful of the older brother's unbalanced behavior. The patient's first vague reference to her childhood terror and fear of this brother became understandable when early memories of the brother's sadistic, and probably sexual, abuse of her as a child broke through in several pictures.

The family background of this patient includes a number of intense traumatic experiences which must have severely disturbed both her childhood and adolescence. It has not been possible to find out how early the mother's alcoholism developed, but it is known that following the father's suicide, the patient also began to drink heavily and became an alcoholic at the age of fifteen. Her alcoholism therefore covered a span of 26 years before she came at the age of 41 for treatment with this therapist.

Miss Elton went to a fashionable finishing school. She later became an extremely able private secretary, but it is known that she was never able to do even the simplest problems in arithmetic. The patient often complained during art therapy sessions about the dullness of the routine of an office secretary; she expressed her sense of superiority to the narrow demands imposed by such work and longed vaguely for something more creative to do. She filled many note-books with a rather chaotic expression of her moods and phantasies. Some of these will be quoted in relation to several of the patient's pictures. At times she admitted that she wrote in her notebook as an escape from having to face the reality of getting a job.

The patient was married and divorced twice. She did not spend much time during the art therapy sessions discussing either of these marriages; they had probably already been fully discussed with the previous therapist. Both of Miss Elton's husbands were alcoholic. When she was planning to divorce her second husband, whom she met through Alcoholics Anonymous, he had, when drunk, forced his way into her apartment and abused her both sexually and physically.

During the 25 years prior to art therapy treatment, Miss Elton had passed through the various types of suffering and degradation generally asso-ciated with severe alcoholism. She had been a member of Alcoholics Anony-mous for some time, but during the art therapy sessions she seemed to be critical of certain aspects of this movement. She had received, at various times, most of the known treatments to relieve alcoholism. During the two previous years prior to the art therapy sessions, she was being treated both medically and psychiatrically by the previous therapist, who was a psychiatrist. She received "Antabuse" treatment, and this seemed to have been successful in terminating her use of alcohol at that time. But the use of small amounts of Dexedrine, which was substituted for the alcohol, led to the patient's increased dependence on this drug; through its overuse Miss Elton became addicted to Dexedrine, taking as much as 20 grams at a time. During the first few art therapy sessions she frequently developed states of visual hallucination and dissociation which, as she later admitted, were induced or intensified by her excessive use of Dexedrine.

Rorschach Test

A Rorschach Test had been given to Miss Elton 26 months before art ther-apy sessions were undertaken. This Rorschach showed the severe personality disturbances of this patient more than two years before she began art therapy. The psychologist stated: "Miss Elton is an extremely intelligent person whose intellectual and creative energies have been turned inward in response to a frightening environment. She is anxious and depressed and is seeking to avoid anxiety by withdrawing into a phantasy world. She is nevertheless in contact with reality and it is suggested that in pressure situations she might resort to suicide as a solution. There are sexual difficulties. Genetic conflicts center about the father-figure toward whom ambivalent feelings are registered. . . . The diagnosis offered is mixed neurosis with strong depressive elements in a mark-edly schizoid personality. The question of whether this is an early schizophrenic state must be raised. At any rate this is certainly a fertile field for the develop-ment of such a reaction."

This remarkably sensitive and accurate Rorschach report was clearly confirmed in the course of the art therapy sessions.

Miss Elton can be categorized in terms of alcoholism as a "primary addict," as confirmed by that leading authority on the treatment of alcoholism, Dr. Ruth Fox. In her description of the primary addict, Dr. Fox states:

> "He is an inadequate, immature person with personality maladjustments started early and was pathological from the start. He has grandiose hopes but has rarely achieved any degree of success in school work, marriage or social life. . . . In summary, we should stress again that alcohol addiction may be a symptom of any underlying personality maladjustment; that the soil in which alcoholism grows is almost always the neurotic character; that this neurotic pattern was formed in infancy or early childhood because of the disturbances in the relationship of the child to the significant persons with whom he came in contact; that the vicissitudes in the early life of an alcoholic are no different from those which underlie neurosis, psychosis or psychopathy, i.e., the choice of symptoms may be influenced by many factors, perhaps both constitutional and environmental; that the egocentricity and immaturity characteristic of the alcoholic may denote a lack of development in the primary addicts. . . ."[2]

In the following report on the development of the art therapy sessions with Miss Elton, the typical characteristics of the primary addict are clearly shown in both the pictures and verbal responses of this alcoholic woman.

An Autobiography by the Patient

Miss Elton had on several occasions referred to an "autobiography" which she had written during treatment by the previous therapist. She said that she was revising it before returning it to him. The present therapist has never seen this document and does not know whether it really exists. On more than one occasion, when forgotten memories of early childhood were recovered in the art therapy session, the patient would say that she must now include this newly recovered material in her "Autobiography."

Irregular Timing of the Art Therapy Sessions

The instability shown by this alcoholic patient during the three trial sessions made it necessary to be extremely flexible about arranging further therapy appointments. Miss Elton's unpredictable behavior made it impossible to plan ahead for a schedule of regular weekly sessions. She was usually late to appointments, coming sometimes a half hour or even an hour and a half late. In order to accomplish anything with this disturbed patient it was necessary to leave the evening free of other appointments, so that whenever she arrived the session could begin. Miss Elton would sometimes telephone for an appointment when she had finished a picture which she wanted to talk about. Due to states of depression, she would sometimes miss an appointment, without telephoning.

---

[2] *Ibid.*, p. 258.

At other times she might not come because she had cut off her hair or because she had no clean dress with which to cover her compulsive scratching and scarring of herself.

In spite of such complications, Miss Elton did develop and improve considerably during the limited period of eleven sessions during a period of two and a half months. There was then no therapy sessions within the next four weeks, while the therapist was on vacation. In the twelfth session, following the therapist's return, Miss Elton showed her a number of quite striking new pictures which she had made during the therapist's absence. An unforeseen new factor had been introduced in the patients life while the therapist was away which led to a sudden termination of the art therapy sessions, after this twelfth session. This will be explained at the conclusion of this study.

Miss Elton's Woman Friend Assists the Therapist

Invaluable assistance in following Miss Elton's erratic behavior was offered by the patient's woman friend. Whenever Miss Elton would telephone to her about some new pictures which she had made, this friend would make notes of the conversation for the therapist. This was especially helpful because the patient often gave her friend the first immediate free associations to her new pictures before she had shown them to the therapist. When talking to her friend, Miss Elton would often quite freely voice her ambivalent feelings toward the present and the former therapist.

Following the third trial session, when Miss Elton had been told that she would be accepted for further art therapy sessions, she telephoned her friend and exposed her unstable and ambivalent feelings; at one moment she spoke to her friend enthusiastically about the art therapy sessions and described the warmth of the therapist's response to her; then a moment later she spoke of her suspicion of the art therapist's ulterior motive in working with her. While she had previously feared her dismissal when the trial sessions were over, she now expressed her masochistic need of punishment by saying, "I almost wish she would say that I can't be helped." Then she would quickly reverse herself and tell her friend, "I hope I'll be accepted so that I can show her my capacity to respond to her demands."

When Miss Elton had been informed that she would be accepted for regular therapy sessions, she commented about this news to her friend over the telephone:

> "I feel a lot better. I don't know what goes on in the way we communicate. I've had so many misconceptions in the past. It was such a nice talk, I don't want to count on it all too much. I'm always going overboard with enthusiasm. Maybe I read things into what she said that weren't there. But she sounded so kind. . . . Maybe it is because she is so kind that she said the things she did. . . . I'm probably just a guinea pig to her. Somebody she wants to gather material on. . . . I completely overdid my visit. I always do. And she was so wonderful about it, I wanted to phone and thank her. . . . I'm lucky to have ever known a person like that.

If she doesn't work with me at least I have known her. [This comment relates to the patient's picture of herself kneeling, surrounded by an explosion" (Fig. 31).] . . . Everything she said helped me to lose my fear. . . . Why isn't everybody kind? How do you suppose she'll tell it to me if she can't work with me? She'll never just come out and say I'm too far gone to be helped. I wish she would. I wish she'd say I can't be helped. . . . But if she would work with me I'd try so hard. I'd do my very best. It would be easy to do my best with her. She brings that out in me."

Fourth Session

"Figure of Myself on a Stage: The Audience Is Dr. G., You and Myself"

This sketch (Fig. 32) was quickly drawn in the presence of the therapist. The central yellow figure on the stage, Miss Elton said, was herself; the two heads on either side of her were "two aspects of myself mocking me; the head on my left is a shadow of me making fun of me; the head on my right, he's trying to frighten me. . . . Out of the darkness monsters are coming from the Grand Union Hotel where I was last with my mother." The outline of the three people below the stage, she said, were "Dr. G., you and myself."

Here the patient has expressed her dissociated state in two ways. On the stage two aspects of herself mock her, and then as audience she watches herself exhibiting herself on the stage—certainly a schizophrenic type of expression.

Fifth Session

"My Two Selves in a Circus: My Tight-rope Picture"

This picture (Fig. 33) was produced at home. In both execution and meaning it represents a surprising development of artistic expression by this patient. Her original intention of again drawing a monster had first, she explained, turned into a net which is still visible beside the dark woman in this picture. She then described the way that, contrary to her original plan, the picture began to change:

> "It's now become my tight-rope picture. It's turned into a circus. I didn't know what that net was when I first showed you the picture last week. And then when I took it home, I made the woman in black. I meant to draw my sister and Dr. G. standing below the net, but then I saw other things. When I made the tight-rope I had trouble putting anyone on it. Then, suddenly somebody nude appeared to me on the tight-rope, swinging one leg happily, with one arm draped around the pole. So I started to draw her. Her back, you see, is turned away from the net and the other woman. I tried to make her with an arm raised, pointing toward the future, but I couldn't draw her that way. She's looking pretty hopeful, pretty up and coming! Underneath, way below, so as to give an idea of the depth and height of an arena in a circus, is only one thing—a chained lion."

Fig. 32.   "Figure of Myself on a Stage: The Audience is Dr. G., You and Myself."

Fig. 33.   "My Two Selves in a Circus: My Tight-rope Picture."

The two women in the picture she then described as two aspects of her-self. "The dead self," she said, "is the dark woman falling from the broken net. The large, nude woman on the tight-rope," she added, "was my new live self, facing toward the future." "The chained lion far below me," she explained, "my previous therapist who had thrown me to the lions." This comment expressed the patient's revived hostility toward the previous therapist who, she now feared, was rejecting his role as a father figure, because he now abandoned her to the new art therapist.

While making this surprisingly complex picture, the patient drew herself in a state of deep depression (the black figure), then transformed herself into the manic state of a "new self" (in the nude figure), where she is being made over by means of art therapy. While making this picture, Miss Elton said that she had again been obsessed with an impulse to chop off her hair; but this time she had succeeded in stopping herself before she had done much of it. Anxiety, while working on this picture, had apparently mobilized a return to her previous form of symbolic self-mutilation. When anxious, she also returned to severe scratching and abrasion of the skin on all parts of her body.

Sixth Session

"The Graveyard, Two Men and a Young Girl"

When Miss Elton showed this picture (Fig. 34) to the therapist, she was very excited. It had, she said, taken her four days to complete. In this drawing she said that she was attempting to bury her former therapist, Dr. G., and her father in the same graveyard: "My blind rage against Dr. G. had started again. . . . I was trying to draw one grave for Dr. G. and one grave for my father. But it wouldn't draw itself." She pointed to the fence and the gate she had drawn for the cemetery. "I had fun," she said, "drawing the angel with the halo. When it's dark in the room, the other figures—monsters around the angel—seem to show." (The vision of monsters about which she hallucinated was evidently the result of another overdose of Dexedrine.)

"The gravedigger in this picture," she continued, "was going to be Dr. G. And this opening was meant to be my father's grave. Dr. G. had dug it up. There was a casket with my father in it. There was a casket open and it was for Dr. G., but it couldn't work." "The girl," she said, "is myself. I'm going to stand there until I know. I am standing there waiting for Dr. G. and Father to be buried." (This patient had never forgiven the father for not sending her, as well as her mother, a message when he committed suicide.) "This girl," she added, "will eventually have this grave with twin caskets, one for Dr. G. and one for my father. But first everything has to be brought up. I'm going to stay there," she said, pointing to herself in the picture, "feet set, and with faith that I'll do it." The patient added, "When I was furious at Dr. G., I jotted down ideas about my father. . . . I have a list of anger pictures planned about father and Dr. G."

This identification of the previous therapist, Dr. G., with her father was clearly expressed a few days earlier. "A lot of this hate," she then said, "is for father and not for Dr. G.; because it's blind and frustrated, it's a terrific strong thing. . . . When the feeling that Dr. G. rejects me takes hold, it reaches far beyond him and there's so much more to it than him. I must try to spot what it is."

"My Brother's Hand"

The patient's fear of her older brother, when she was a child, is depicted in this upraised and threatening hand (Fig. 35). This sketch brought back a rush of childhood memories which were projected in the next pictures.

"The Red Stocking and the Mouse"

This is the drawing (Fig. 36) of a recurrent dream which the patient said she had experienced since she was five years old. Everything in this picture

Fig. 34.   "The Graveyard, Two Men and a Young Girl."

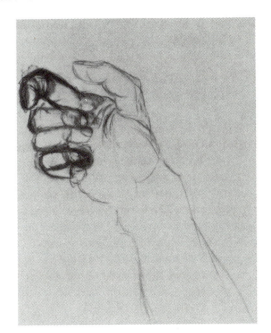

Fig. 35. "My Brother's Hand."

Fig. 36. "The Red Stocking and the Mouse." Color plate on page xiii.

was drawn in pencil except the important red stocking. The story of this dream, as described by the patient, was in two parts: the middle right section dealt with the patient as a child of five eating at a table as her older brother stood beside her. "He is always, in this picture, beckoning . . . like a bogy man of the worst type. . . ." At the bottom of the staircase in the second part of her dream picture she drew a small mouse. The patient then explained:

> "I rushed down the staircase past the mouse; it was like being between Scylla and Charybdis. Terrific fear! We used to hang up long stockings at Christmas time. This red stocking is empty. This dream memory comes back over and over. Why should I remember that beckoning finger of my brother? I want to do a full page of this picture. I want to do a brilliant stocking. The word 'outrage' comes to me. A soiled stocking, baggy at the knee. I'm terrified of the mouse in the dream but I'm not scared of mice, actually, but of bugs and insects. . . . My brother went into every refinement of sadism. He was always telling me how ugly, stupid and clumsy I was and I believed these things. It was mental cruelty. He squeezed my fingernails until it hurt. Both my brothers did that."

At this time the patient remained unconscious of the sexual symbolism of this dream. But later, when the penis symbol of the red stocking reappeared spontaneously in a number of other pictures which followed, she became aware of its symbolic meaning.

The Patient as a Baby on Her Doctor's Lap

This drawing (Fig. 37) shows a vision that the patient had experienced when her previous therapist had gone on vacation. "I had so much transference to Dr. G. that he was surprised. This picture isn't drawn quite the way I saw it. The baby, myself, on Dr. G.'s lap would have been as big as I am. The worst thing about this baby was that she was in no way precocious. I first saw this picture when Dr. G. was on his vacation. As I got off the doctor's lap, it (the baby) came inside of me, faster than I could shove it away. The baby has a will to grow but nowhere to go. It's impossible for it to grow while it's on the doctor's lap. The other me can't grow while the baby is there on his lap. Outwardly, I was going to see if I couldn't get off his lap. Back of the baby is a pink mass which drew itself."

While the patient did not recognize that the pink mass was the beginning of the form of her adult self which now wished to get off the doctor's lap, she had nevertheless unconsciously projected it. She was also unconscious of having drawn the doctor with a black skin. She was startled when, some weeks later, she became aware of this. She was then able to associate the dark skin which she had given the doctor with the dark skin of a Negro who, in her later recall of childhood memories, she felt had probably seduced her when she was a small child in the South.

As in the picture "The Graveyard," Miss Elton had here again identified her former psychiatrist with her father. Here she regressed to an infantile state seeking to be loved, but there is also the hint in the incomplete pink form which she drew of her growing self that as she became more mature she would be able at a future time to get off her doctor's lap and become more adult.

"Pig with Its Throat Cut, Spurting Blood"

This drawing (Fig. 38) was another childhood memory of hog killing in the South which the patient said that she had seen when she was seven years old. "When they plunge the knife in the pig," she explained, "the blood spurts. When I told my father what I'd seen, he said that I was blood-thirsty. I was very upset at that. It wasn't so. . . . The pig I drew is really a monster—myself. You see, above the pig there's a hand holding him." She explained that this hand was her own. "It's a struggle between the pig and me and I'm going to win."

Seventh Session

"Myself As a Child in Bed with a Pig Monster: a Dream"

"This," said the patient, "is a dream I had of myself in bed with the monster (Fig. 39). The monster was drawn first. I was only done afterwards. I didn't know what I was doing; it drew itself. I had this dream as a phantasy; that's why I had one eye open and one eye closed. I was first an animal or monster shaking the bars until I frightened myself. The little girl came after I'd drawn the monster. This thing," she said, pointing to the monster's penis, "drew itself. I knew I had no business taking it out of the picture since it drew itself." She then asked the therapist, "Do you remember the picture 'The Red Stocking and

Fig. 37. The Patient as a Baby on Her Doctor's Lap. Color plate on page xiv.

the Mouse'? I have a feeling there may be a tie-up between this new picture and the Red Stocking one." Miss Elton then recalled, "I used the word 'outrage' then about my memories of my brother, connected with that Red Stocking picture. I see now that the red stocking must have been a penis just like the one on this pig monster. It makes me feel that my older brother may have seduced me when I was five years old. The door at the back of this picture relates to the one in the Red Stocking picture. I had a feeling of terror as I lay in bed with this monster." (The pig form of this monster shows a direct association with the previous picture of "Pig with its Throat Cut, Spurting Blood.")

One Black Monster Drawing

This "large grinning monster" (Fig. 40) was described by the patient as a prostitute. "See," she said, "the dissolute expression of the drunken woman who considers herself a prostitute. She is syphilitic, laughing like hell at anybody who dares say she is going to pieces." Another picture, with a jumble of broken

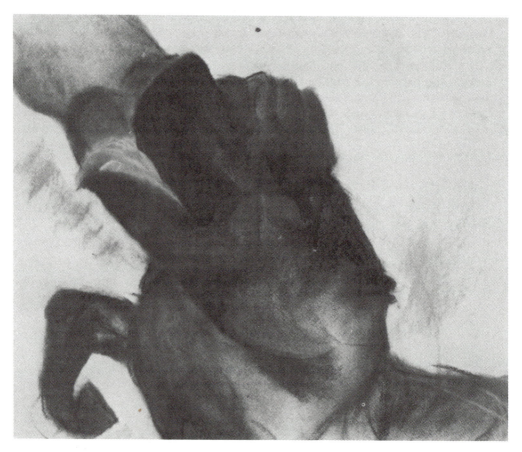

Fig. 38. "Pig with Its Throat Cut, Spurting Blood."

Fig. 39.   "Myself As a Child in Bed with
a Pig Monster: a Dream."

Fig. 40.   One Black Monster Drawing.

heads and bodies (not shown) was meant to represent the degradation, horror and despair that the patient had known when she was drunk in the past.

"Myself with a Rope Around Me" (First scribble drawing)

This drawing (Fig. 41a) was the result of the patient's first attempt to use the scribble technique. In such a projection of spontaneous zig-zag, curving and crossing lines, the patient had been encouraged to use a scribble like a Rorschach ink blot in order to discover symbols or images within its form. In this first attempt at a scribble drawing it is evident that the patient phantasied her own self-destruction.

"Dr. G. and Me" (Scribble)

This second scribble drawing (Fig. 41b) repeats the theme of the drawing in which the patient was on the doctor's lap as a baby (Fig. 37). Miss Elton's only comment was, "It's the same old thing."

Eighth Session

"Memory of Myself Visiting Mother in an Insane Asylum"

In this picture (Fig. 42) Miss Elton recalled a particular visit that she had made to her mother at a mental institution. The patient explained that the figure in brown was herself; the figure of the girl in the center was, she said, "an insane girl that I saw rotting in a dark room alone. The doctors were giving this patient the hot box. I thought her face was kind of pitiful. This drawing began to be a picture of my visit to my mother. I made her again in that magenta gown she wore long ago. But later the figure of my mother changed into a monstrous and threatening creature with hoofs. The face of my mother changed into a monster—insanity. Now the picture represents my own fear of insanity." At this particular time the patient was having frequent hallucinations from excessive use of Dexedrine.

Ninth Session

"Things in Me That Want to Be Wretched and Rot"

In this drawing (Fig. 43) made after the previous one of the Insane Asylum, she has drawn herself as a mad-eyed young woman sitting opposite two leering dark figures robed in red. The title that she gave this picture, "Things in Me That Want to Be Wretched and Rot," expressed her own great dread of insanity. On the figure of a young girl she has placed long red stockings reminiscent of the Red Stocking and Mouse Dream Picture (Fig. 36).

Patient's Recognition of the Positive Value of Art Therapy

As Miss Elton's pictures became increasingly expressive of her own growth and development, she was able to verbalize her recognition of the value of art therapy. "I found out that once you've let hate out when you are making pictures, then the hate gets all used up by the time I've finished drawing."

Fig. 41a. "Myself with a Rope Around Me" (First scribble drawing).

Fig. 41b. "Dr. G. and Me" (Scribble),

Fig. 42.   "Memory of Myself Visiting
Mother in an Insane Asylum."
Color plate on page xv.

Fig. 43.   "Things in Me That Want to Be
Wretched and Rot." Color plate
on page xiv.

The patient was then able, after two and a half months of art therapy, to explain to the sister who was assisting her financially how the art therapy sessions had been able to help her:

"Every day I feel better in a new and more stable way. It is a sign of improved health that I'm now able to arrive on my own at a decision and feel it is worth defending.

"In one of your letters you were sweet enough to express sympathy for the disappointment I must feel because of my inability to achieve 'total' health. Disappointment is a mild word because I knew I couldn't remain static and if I was unable to get better I was almost sure to get worse. But I can say now, with what I believe is realistic optimism, that I'm on my way to a state of well-being (happy rather than total) in which I shan't need crutches in order to assume and discharge my responsibilities.

"My starting to mend is undeniably a result of Art Therapy. This work was immediately helpful and its effects are so positive that no one seeing either the pictures or me retains any doubt about its being right for me.

"Before I started with Miss N. I had bogged down to the extent I dreaded life and felt your entire investment might be wasted. When an alcoholic has stopped constructive growing it is seldom he remains sober. I'm now increasingly able to translate experiences into active expression instead of, as often previously, thinking one way and behaving in a contradictory way. My life has been proof enough that words have slight influence on the part of me that dictates my actions. My drawings, though, are sometimes near blueprints of my motivations and thus do affect my actions.

"At this point I won't go into Miss N.'s methods, but if you're ever curious later on you can see some of my pictures. But I would like to say that the only 'achievement' with which Art Therapy concerns itself is health and the achievement of becoming one's true self. Art simply connotes treatment through pictures as well as words. The patient draws pictures of fears, loves, hates—many of which elude the definitions necessary to capture them in words, whether the pictures are good art or bad art. No mastery of formal technique is required to give a glimpse inside oneself that is more accurate and more deeply suggestive than words usually are; and pictures are impervious to distortion in a way words rarely are. Sometimes a picture suggests yet another, and soon one is drawing the shapes of things one had not been conscious of before, but which none-the-less are crippling. Drawings may expose disturbances in the very process of doing one in; eagerly one draws, until the trouble's hidden nature is sufficiently revealed to be dealt with adequately. There has been no need to fumble unfamiliar words nor chance the confusion so often caused by cloudy definitions."

Miss Elton had explained in the last part of the letter to her sister that because of illness she had been unable to pay the therapist as she had intended. She then thanked the sister for her financial assistance to cover her rent and food, but she made no reference to the fact that it was due to the efforts of the present and former therapists that the patient had received funds from her sister. This was done in spite of the fact that Miss Elton had insisted that her sister should not be told of her financial problems.

When Miss Elton's sister, in response to the patient's enthusiastic description of her art therapy sessions, offered to pay for them, the patient refused this offer. She gave two reasons for this refusal: First, she insisted that she intended to pay the therapist later (but she never did this). Second, she explained that since she intended eventually to do art therapy herself with alcoholics, she would then need more money from her sister for her later training.

In her contradictory responses, Miss Elton had expressed several of the typical attitudes of an alcoholic. While she had been able in her letter to her sister to give an unusually intelligent and appreciative expression concerning the value of her own art therapy experience with the present therapist, she had simultaneously turned her hostility against this therapist by refusing to let her sister pay what was already owed the therapist. Thus Miss Elton expressed her ambivalence toward the therapist by praising what she had gained through art therapy but refusing to have it paid for by the sister, and then arguing that the sister's money must be saved for her own future training as an art therapist, when she would then be able to compete with the present therapist.

Crisis in the Art Therapy Sessions

At this juncture, Miss Elton became increasingly hostile and arrogant toward the therapist, criticizing her for having told the sister about her financial difficulties. The therapist was therefore obliged to challenge the patient about her contradictory behavior in welcoming the money sent by the sister and then criticizing both therapists who had obtained it for her. Miss Elton was told that since she was behaving so unreasonably with the therapist about the money she received from the sister, it would be better to stop the art therapy sessions immediately. Next morning a contrite Miss Elton telephoned in a chastened mood, and since her unreasonable arrogance had subsided, the art therapy sessions were resumed.

Tenth Session

Development of the "My Universe" Picture: First Version

The title of this drawing, "My Universe" (Fig. 44), was based upon a previous comment by the therapist which the patient had not forgotten—namely, that she ought some day to make pictures that dealt with her own immediate universe. This drawing, as the patient explained, dealt with her hostile feelings toward both therapists who had just obtained money for her from the sister. Miss Elton explained that she had pictured herself with only her head floating on the water in the pool. (It is noteworthy that here she represents herself with three heads.) Above her floating head she had drawn figures of her sister and both her previous and present therapists. The picture is somber except for the brightness of the sympathetic sunlight surrounding the sister. She has drawn the former therapist in a boy-like sailor suit. This apparently symbolized his naval activities somewhat mockingly, because the patient could not see him while he was away.

Miss Elton had described in detail to her woman friend what a difficult time she had in doing the central figure of the present therapist. She told her, "The figure of M.N. was all out of proportion to my sister's and Dr. G.'s—so much bigger. I first made her form square and defiant looking: I wanted to draw her face with that set, firm expression she gets when she's mad at me and beats my ears back. But M.N.'s head just wouldn't get right, so I rubbed it out and left her headless." She laughed as she said this. "When I started drawing Dr. G. and my sister, they suddenly turned into trees, bearing fruit. The fruit on my sister's tree was white and the fruit on Dr. G.'s tree was black. And when I went back to poor headless M.N., believe it or not, she too turned into a tree! But her tree bore fruit of all colors."

While explaining to the therapist during the art therapy session about the unexpected transformations that occurred as she drew this picture, she did not hesitate to tell the therapist about her decapitation. About this picture Miss Elton was now less vehement in expressing the hostility which she had intended against the therapist. She admitted, however, that contrary to her original wish to distort the therapist's figure, she had found that the large and dominant form of the therapist had "drawn itself." She told the therapist that "this unintended transformation of your figure is, you know, a great compliment to you."

Fig. 44. Development of the "My Universe" Picture: First Version. Color plate on page xv.

Eleventh Session

Another Pencil Drawing for the "Universe" Pictures

The jumble of faces and animals in this picture (Fig. 45) was again influenced by excessive use of Dexedrine, yet each form had symbolic significance to the patient. The nude woman drawn in the center was, she said, herself, again rising out of the waters of the pool. Here Miss Elton said that she had drawn her own head looking at the mother's breast as it was held in the hand of the kneeling mother. About this mother image the patient remarked, "I don't seem to be disturbed now as I look at mother's breast."

All the monsters and creatures surrounding the patient's nude figure represent, she explained, symbols of early childhood experiences. The multicolored bird at the bottom of the picture, she said, was a vulture, a bird that protected her. The cock on top of the picture reminded her of the cocks that her second brother raised for cock fighting; he forced her to watch these fights which she hated. She pointed also to the reappearance of the red stocking symbol, now drawn with a face inside the stocking. Two creatures near the cock caused Miss Elton to query whether her early sexual experience had not been connected with her older brother. "The mouse with divided head," observed the patient, "is split in two like me."

A number of the symbols in the previous drawing were repeated in another picture (not shown) which included a vulture, a pig-monster, the red stocking,

Fig. 45.   Another Pencil Drawing for the "Universe" Picture.

the mouse and a scarcely discernible figure of the patient rising out of a pool. This chaotic sketch also showed the influence of Dexedrine.

Growing Physical and Emotional Improvement in the Patient's Condition

Miss Elton appeared to be more relaxed and happier after eleven weeks of art therapy. She joked about her improved condition, saying that she was afraid she was getting well, since for the first time she was now able to get up in the morning and enjoy the fresh air. The patient seemed gayer and there was a hopeful expression in her eyes. Her close friend remarked that in the ten years that she had known her, Miss Elton had never looked so well. The habitual scratching of her skin had diminished. Another sign of the patient's improved condition was her determination to seek medical assistance in order to overcome her Dexedrine addiction while the therapist was on vacation.

Communications from the Patient while the Therapist was on Vacation

The first communication from Miss Elton which reached the therapist while on vacation was a postcard saying, "My deepest thanks for lowering your rope to me down the cliff side." Here again there reappeared the cliff symbol that had always meant so much to the patient. The second communication from Miss Elton was a long-distance telephone call toward the end of the therapist's vacation. She sounded hopeful and in good spirits and said that she was eager to show the pictures made during the therapist's absence. The treatment to relieve her Dexedrine addiction, she reported, was after some delay about to begin.

Twelfth and Final Session

All of the following pictures were drawn during the therapist's vacation.

"The Black Elm Tree": Subtitled "My Universe Now"

This elm tree (Fig. 46), Miss Elton explained, showed a night scene on the lawn of her childhood home in the South. "I went back there again with mother before we were penniless. . . . There is darkness behind the picture. The tree is black. The sky is stormy, but it begins to lighten. I drew my black tree between 1:00 and 3:00 P.M., just when you went on vacation. Then I cleaned and fixed it up all the next day."

"My Rock with Vulture and M.N.'s Reflected Universe"

Again in this quite beautiful picture (Fig. 47), the three fruit trees of different colors were assigned symbolically to the sister and the two therapists. Miss Elton explained, "Here I am rising out of the pool and facing toward the rock on which rest my vulture and my orange and yellow disk; this small disk represents my own universe." The patient's left arm is seen holding onto this rock above the water, while her right arm rests on the multicolored disk in the pool; this second larger disk, the patient said, "symbolizes your universe. It's what I'm trying to create in myself . . . your inner security, your inner freedom and integration; obviously I'm not there yet. I'm trying, in this picture, to leave you to go to my own place. In the first 'Universe' picture I was leaning on you. Now I'm trying to get on my own. That's the meaning of 'The Rock and the Vulture.' The vulture comes to my aid in time of distress. He is symbolic of what I'm trying to find in myself. When the red stocking gets too much for me, when things get too rough, the vulture protects me. The vulture's feathers have the same colors as the fruit of your tree." The patient was especially happy at the creation of this picture, which showed her growing integration and growing freedom from dependence on the therapist.

"M.N. Is Dancing with a Tree: and I am in the Pool, Holding to Her Reflected Universe"

Here (Fig. 48) the patient has drawn herself again in the pool, clinging to the trunk of a tree in what she described as the therapist's "reflected universe." Pointing to herself in the pool, she expressed self-pity about "poor me below." The branches above the water again bear multicolored fruit. She mentioned that some weeks before the therapist's return she had told her woman friend that she meant to express her hostility against the therapist in this final "Universe" picture, but that again the picture "drew itself differently." Why Miss Elton had eventually drawn the therapist in a multicolored gown dancing with a tree was not, unfortunately, explained in this final hurried session. Had the therapist been able to see the patient even once more, the deeper symbolic meaning of this and the other pictures might have been obtained from the patient.

"An Empty Couch"

"This couch made of horsehair" (Fig. 49), she said, "recalls my older brother and sexual things. This couch is where my brother suffocated me. Impact on my masochism comes through, too." In her next picture she drew "My Brother Bent Back My Fingernails" (not shown).

My Older Brother Doing the Doctor Jekyll and Mr. Hyde Business"

"My older brother would," she said, "come up to the third floor when I was little and alone. And he'd frighten me, doing the Dr. Jekyll and Mr. Hyde, until I screamed" (Fig. 50).

"On the Couch"

The patient said that in this picture (Fig. 51) she was, as a little girl, lying on a couch with a man. Her associations to this drawing were: "A man . . . memory of seduction . . . red stocking . . . penis. I see I am able to draw the truth. I am saved by the reflection of M.N.'s tree picture. It steadied me looking at it. The man hasn't the face of my brother. I've been having a bad time with Dexedrine."

"On the Couch Again"

"This" (Fig. 52), she said, "continues the previous memories of seduction."

Fig. 46.   "The Black Elm Tree": Sub-
          titled "My Universe Now."

Fig. 47.   "My Rock with Vulture and
          M.N.'s Reflected Universe."
          Color plate on page xvii.

Fig. 48.   "M.N. Is Dancing with a Tree: and I am in the Pool, Holding to Her Reflected Universe." Color plate on page xviii.

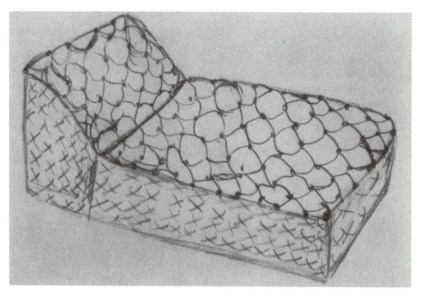

Fig. 49.   "An Empty Couch."

"Four Corpses in a Hospital": a Dream

In the patient's dream (Fig. 53) she was walking down a steep path and in the distance were trees, mountains and beauty. In trying to reach this beauty she said that she walked down a path and came to a hospital. The door of the hospital was open and the lesbian friend who was with her told her to look in. She saw there four hospital beds with people in them "who were dead—and very dead. When I tried to draw this dream, the corpse in the last bed had turned out to be me staring horror-stricken at the colored man of my memory who seduced me at five years of age; he was staring obscenely."

Young Woman Carrying Two Pails

No explanation was given of this picture (Fig. 54). The body build of this figure resembles that of the patient. The diagonal line separates the woman's body and this division is emphasized by the darkness of the upper part of the figure, while the lower part is bright. In another session an interpretation of this picture might have been obtained from the patient. It suggests two things: that the patient feels the weight of carrying the burden of living, and the possible split in her own personality.

"My Conscience"

This symbolic design (Fig. 55) was the next to the last picture drawn before the therapist's return. In this and the following picture Miss Elton was expressing the anguish which a review of her wasted and futile life had caused her.

Fig. 50. "My Older Brother Doing the Doctor Jekyll and Mr. Hyde Business."

Fig. 51.   "On the Couch."

Fig. 52.   "On the Couch Again."

Fig. 53.   "Four Corpses in a Hospital": a Dream.

Fig. 54.   Young Woman Carrying Two Pails.

Fig. 55.   "My Conscience."
          Color plate on page xvi.

"Here," the patient explained, "I am stretched out on the floor at the bottom of the picture. I'm bound by my conscience; that's the black material around my waist." She draws the therapist's attention to how she has drawn her legs covered with red sores from scratching her skin. The patient pointed to the red stocking that hung from the purple monster's mouth and said, "That's the monster's tongue; it's dripping blood." Here Miss Elton has again recalled her childhood memories of seduction, in this tongue-penis-red stocking image. She also explained the lapel pin which the monster wore; she called it "a maypole lapel pin. Each string on the maypole," she said, "is a noose; each represents what I put myself through. The center figure represents me drinking; the second figure on the left shows me skating on thin ice; in the third figure I'm praying. The fourth, on the right, shows where the monster has thrown me onto the side."

"Join the Maypole Dance"

Miss Elton called this picture (Fig. 56) "Another maypole with ribbons . . . their magenta color shows it's basically the robe of my conscience." (This magenta was the mother's color, a superego symbol used unconsciously by the patient for her conscience.)

Each of the maypole ribbons is, according to the patient, tied to a review of some aspect of her life. The woman in the upper section, lying supine in the sexual embrace of a brown monster, with long red tongue, was interpreted as "a bit of Sodom with a schmoo. It's symbolical," she added, "of my two husbands. I thought that by now I would be free of Dexedrine, but I wasn't, so I tried to figure out ways of punishing myself. This picture again relates to my conscience." Pointing to the woman half kneeling in the lower corner, she said, "That's me getting up. The man always flipped at the genitals." He turned out to be the same man as on the couch (Fig. 51) and in the picture, "Four Corpses in a Hospital" (Fig. 53). The vague blue form on the central ribbon was described by the patient as "a blue fetus, maybe me. Such a baby—going on." The yellow-green shape on the ribbon to the right she called simply "formless."

These last two pictures were drawn after further unexpected postponement of medical help for the treatment of her Dexedrine addiction. In drawing these two devastating surveys of her life, Miss Elton showed, even in her depressed state, a growing ego strength in daring to review the ways in which she had failed.

At the following session the therapist had expected to obtain from the patient further interpretation of these thirteen pictures, but Miss Elton canceled the next appointment and the therapist was informed only some months later, by a mutual friend, that Miss Elton had married the refugee physician who had eventually treated her for Dexedrine addiction. She had, indeed, as she had said in describing the "Rock and Vulture" picture, proved that her trying to leave the therapist had succeeded while the therapist was on vacation. The woman friend lost contact with this alcoholic patient when she went West after her third marriage.

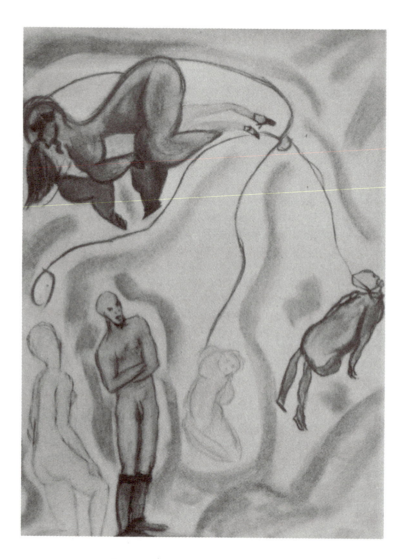

Fig. 56. "Join the Maypole Dance."

CONCLUSION

The life of this intelligent, 41-year-old alcoholic woman was from its inception a tragic one. The disruptive factors in her family had their roots in the early years of her life and were severe enough to have unbalanced an even stronger personality than Miss Elton's. The patient was naturally unaware in childhood of the cause of the mounting strains in the family setting, but the suicide of the father when she was an adolescent left her responsible for her unbalanced alcoholic mother who was later committed to an asylum. Miss Elton's recollections of being frightened and maltreated by her sadistic brothers in childhood added to her difficult early history.

As Miss Elton became able to express herself more freely in the creation of spontaneous images, many early memories, as well as hallucinations, were released. One of the most surprising was her unconscious drawing of her previous therapist as being black, as she phantasied herself sitting on his lap as a baby. Until some weeks later, she did not realize that she had drawn her psychiatrist as a Negro. When she realized this, a flood of childhood memories of her life in the South came back to her. Among them was a feeling that as a small child she had been seduced by a Negro. Other images of possible seduction by one of her probably alcoholic brothers came out also in several drawings about her childhood (Figs. 35, 39, 49-52).

Given her pathological family history, it is not surprising that Miss Elton lived a life weighted with disaster. Her chronic alcoholism began early in life and led her into two unhappy marriages to alcoholics; she experienced all forms of degradation known to alcoholics and tried various forms of treatment. During a two-year period, before beginning the art therapy sessions, she had received Antabuse, which had successfully terminated her use of alcohol but had left her dependent on Dexedrine as a substitute. The patient's continuing Dexedrine addiction was an important factor in releasing her hallucinations during the art therapy sessions.

In spite of Miss Elton's instability and hallucinatory visions which were projected in some of her pictures, marked improvement in her emotional behavior and physical health was shown. Her friend of ten years was much encouraged by the modifications in the patient's appearance and more steady responses to life after two and a half months of art therapy.

In retrospect, the art therapist's separation of four weeks from the patient left the patient emotionally at loose ends. Her own intention to use this period of the therapist's absence to try to overcome her dependence on Dexedrine seemed praiseworthy. But what could not be foreseen was that the young refugee physician who treated her for Dexedrine addiction would abuse his medical responsibility by marrying her so suddenly. It was not surprising, therefore, to be informed some months later that the patient's sudden marriage had run into some serious difficulties.

III. ART THERAPY IN THE TREATMENT OF A DEPRESSED WOMAN

Mrs. Arnstein was a 55-year-old woman of German-Jewish extraction who suffered from a deep depression. Prior to her art therapy sessions she had undergone analytic psychotherapy with a well-known psychoanalyst. It was on the advice of this analyst that she made an appointment to see the art therapist. The psychoanalyst proposed to continue seeing the patient on a reduced schedule when she began art therapy sessions, which he felt might help alleviate her problems.

The Patient's History

The following letter about Mrs. Arnstein was sent by the psychoanalyst to the art therapist before she met the patient:

> "This patient came to see me in a profound depression masked by insomnia, plus painful symptoms of diverticulitis. With the initial relief from insomnia, the depression naturally and inevitably deepened at first, and the intestinal symptoms became more severe. Then, as the underlying depression cleared, the intestinal symptoms disappeared almost entirely.

> "There is in the background a tragic and painful life story, having to do with the death of this patient's husband in a skiing accident, and the murder of her older daughter, her son-in-law and her grandchild by the Nazis. Her younger daughter, who came to this country with her mother some years before the war, is married to a young European psychiatrist who was trained in this country. Her son is a research chemist and lives in Germany.

> "The double tragedy in this woman's life began with the death of her husband in a skiing accident, leaving her alone to bring up three young children. Some years later, after her emigration to the United States with her younger daughter, there occurred the tragic death of her older daughter, her son-in-law and grandchild in a concentration camp in Ger-

many. These two extremely traumatic experiences preceded the development of the patient's deep depression."

The analyst described Mrs. Arnstein as "an intelligent, intellectual woman with a broad interest in and knowledge of art."

Why This Patient Wished to Try Art Therapy

At the time when Mrs. Arnstein came to her preliminary appointment with the art therapist, on the advice of the psychoanalyst, she was still an unusually handsome woman with a sensitive but suffering expression. Her most striking feature was a pair of unusually clear blue eyes.

As soon as the therapist had explained how art therapy might supplement her work with the psychoanalyst, she said that she would like to begin immediately. Her motive for undertaking art therapy was, she explained, in order to improve her own artistic expression. She seemed unconcerned about its therapeutic possibilities.

In the first session, Mrs. Arnstein spoke briefly about the double tragedy in her life, the death of her husband in a ski accident and the murder of part of her family by the Nazis. She spent most of the session explaining her artistic interests. She spoke enthusiastically of her great love of flowers and of her particular knowledge and understanding of all forms of art, both ancient and modern. She also informed the therapist of her exceptional taste in clothes as well as art.

Mrs. Arnstein began art therapy with biweekly sessions of an hour and a half, while continuing weekly twenty-minute appointments with the psychoanalyst. As the art therapy sessions progressed, the visits to the analyst were reduced to once a month or even once every six weeks.

THE EARLY SESSIONS

In the early art therapy sessions Mrs. Arnstein had great difficulty in developing spontaneous art expression as well as in obtaining free associations to her pictures. At first she seemed quite tense as she drew her first naïve pictures of pretty flowers, and her conversation was monotonously repetitious as she complained about how "childish," "silly" and "awful" all her pictures were. As she continued to turn her own suppressed rage about her life against her drawings, the therapist asked her whether she could not make a picture expressive of the intense rage that she was feeling against her inadequate pictures. To this suggestion she replied, "The colors of these pastels are so beautiful that I would rather make lovely flowers with them."

Another typical attitude of this patient in the beginning sessions was one of helpless passivity. She would persist in asking the therapist what she should draw. When she was urged each time to decide on a subject for herself, she would protest by insisting again and again, "It would be useless for me to try to draw anything, because all real artists are born and can't be made." The therapist would then assure her that this was not so and that many people who had never drawn before had become able to learn to express their own feelings in spontaneous pictures. For the first five sessions Mrs. Arnstein refused to accept this as a possible goal for herself, so she continued to draw stilted and self-conscious pictures. In the sixth session, however, when the first release of her great suffering emerged in a touching design, profound changes began to take place in her creative expression.

Modification of the Art Therapy Approach

As Mrs. Arnstein was defensively rigid and insecure in her first attempts at drawing spontaneous pictures, the usual procedures of art therapy had to be modified. Like other depressed patients she had repressed the painful experiences of her life and was fearful of exposing them in any spontaneous pictures. Since her motivation in coming to the art therapy sessions was based on a wish to learn how to draw, it was necessary to begin by offering her some of the drawing techniques that she desired. It was hoped that this approach would help reduce her immediate insecurity.

When the patient brought in a still-life drawing of a dish of fruit, she was angry with herself, because as she said, "I can't make the dish lie down." Similarly she became indignant when her drawing of a pitcher looked flat and she could not give it a rounded form. From such practical failures in drawing pictures at home, the art therapy sessions became at first, to a considerable extent, a series of demonstration art lessons on how to improve the patient's efforts to make pictures. These early art sessions were an attempt to build some ego strength in the patient by offering her practical assistance in improving her early pictures. How the problem of perspective, the development of plastic form, and the problem of foreground and background development as well as color relations were dealt with as the patient struggled to improve her drawings will be described and illustrated in relation to a few of her first pictures.

In meeting the immediate demands of this patient to obtain assistance in art expression, it was hoped that she would gain the emotional security to dare to release some of her long-repressed and painful life experiences into really spontaneous pictures. After a month's time, in the sixth art therapy session the patient's inhibitions were reduced to the point where she broke through for the first time with a poignant picture about her tragic life.

Mrs. Arnstein's original resistance to the art therapy sessions had been expressed in the second session, when she asked the art therapist whether it was not wrong for her to spend money on herself in going for psychoanalytic and art therapy sessions at a time (during World War II) when the Red Cross needed the money. To this hypothetical question the art therapist replied that money was not the only way to help and that she did not believe one could really help others until one had straightened oneself out first. The therapist also reminded the patient that if she felt the art therapy sessions were a waste of money she should certainly not continue them. Although Mrs. Arnstein would occasionally refer to doubts about spending her money, a typical response of a depressed patient, she would eventually overcome her resistance and continue the art therapy sessions.

Two Conferences between the Patient's Therapists

The first conference between the psychoanalyst and the art therapist about Mrs. Arnstein occurred over the telephone. The psychoanalyst then discussed the patient's expression of ambivalence toward the therapist during the first two sessions. He said that it was good that the patient's feelings toward the art therapist had come out immediately. It had enabled him, the analyst explained, to get the patient to face for the first time the nature of her resistance to discussing her mother with him. It was now possible for him to show her that she was projecting on to the art therapist, as a woman, her long repressed ambivalent feelings about her mother. As soon as the analyst had been able to make the patient aware of this cause of her resistance to the art therapist, the art therapy sessions proceeded more easily. The combined efforts of a male and female therapist helped to encourage the patient's transference to both a father and a mother figure.

In the first conference with the psychoanalyst the art therapist spoke of her difficulty in getting the patient to talk about her pictures. The analyst said that he also had the same problem with the patient. In fact, he added that Mrs. Arnstein would frequently sit through an entire therapy session without speaking. The art therapist then realized that although she was unable as yet to obtain any free associations from the patient to her early pictures, Mrs. Arnstein did at least speak of her wish to learn to draw and also expressed herself constantly in angry words about the childishness of her efforts to make pictures.

Mrs. Arnstein insisted to the art therapist that the reason she had refused to show the analyst any of her pictures was because her drawings were too "awful" and "childish" for him to see. In order therefore to keep the analyst informed of how the art therapy sessions were proceeding, the therapist brought the patient's pictures to these first conferences. With the strengthening of the transference to both parental figures, Mrs. Arnstein became fearful that the two therapists would compare notes about her, afraid that it might reduce her standing with each of them. This was the reason that the two therapists at first met without her knowledge. Four months later, however, when the patient felt more secure in her relationship to both therapists, she would become impatient if the two did not consult together about her progress as often as she wanted them to.

The advantage of the combined treatment of this depressed patient through the joint efforts of a male psychoanalyst and a female art therapist soon proved its usefulness, for as the patient developed a simultaneous transference to the therapists of both sexes, she was able to release much unconscious material about the pattern of her early family life. This case refutes the doubts sometimes voiced by psychotherapists as to whether the creation of a split transference in the patient might not interfere with treatment. In this case, the double transference proved decidedly helpful.

Mrs. Arnstein's dissatisfaction with her early pictures made her constantly wish to destroy them. It was with difficulty that the art therapist persuaded her that saving her pictures in a portfolio would be of assistance in following her development during the art therapy sessions.

THE EARLY PICTURES

Flowers with Black Centers

In the first session the patient made two flower pictures. The first one (Fig. 57) is shown. When she had drawn this picture she said that she hated it. Another early drawing was the patient's attempt to create her crude idea of a modern abstract design. She disliked it also and again wanted to destroy the picture. (The patient remained completely unconscious of the extent of sexual symbolism in both these drawings.)

The patient became more friendly and relaxed in the art therapy sessions after the psychoanalyst had helped her to understand that the cause of her original resistance to the art therapist had been due to the patient's unconscious identification of the art therapist with her mother, but Mrs. Arnstein was never able to speak of this directly to the art therapist.

When the patient came to the third art therapy session ahead of time, she announced that she had had no lunch and would like some fruit before she began to work. When she had been given fruit, cheese and crackers, she thanked the therapist and explained apologetically that it was most unusual for her to ask anyone for anything. Mrs. Arnstein remained quite unaware of the fact that

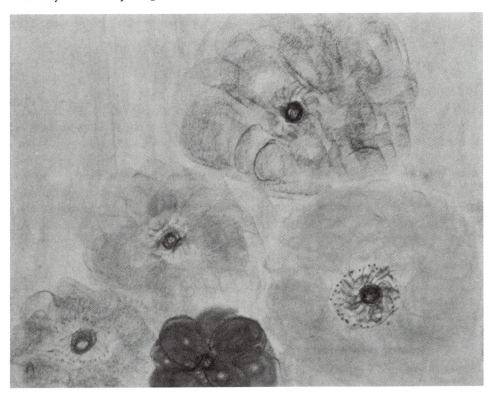

Fig. 57. Flowers with Black Centers.

in asking to be fed by the therapist she was unconsciously testing whether the therapist had now become a good and sustaining mother instead of a hostile one.

In an awkward picture (not shown), the patient transferred her aggression against the Blue Pitcher with Flowers picture onto the pastels by saying, "I hate these pastels; please give me some oil paints instead." She was told that there was nothing wrong with the pastels, but only with her inability to use them in the right way. She was then given a demonstration of the various ways in which the pastels could be applied. As she became familiar with their use, she never asked again for paints.

Frequently, the patient did not really listen to what she was told, but drove ahead compulsively in order to force some quick results. When her haste and tension in making a picture was criticized, she argued that working quickly had made her feel better.

In a second drawing of this same Blue Pitcher with Flowers, the patient was able to apply what she was beginning to learn about the simplification of the flower forms as well as the shaping of the pitcher by a more harmonious use of color.

Throughout these early sessions the art therapist continuously had to counter Mrs. Arnstein's obsessive ambition to succeed immediately with her drawings by reminding her that the goal of the art therapy sessions was not to achieve great art, but to channel her buried feelings into significant pictorial expression.

Fourth Session

The Upright Plate of Fruit

Mrs. Arnstein brought in this picture of a dish of fruit (Fig. 58) that she had drawn at home. She was critical and annoyed that she had been unable to make the plate lie down flat and could not get the fruit to look round. (The picture, as reproduced, has been somewhat improved with the advice of the therapist, so that the drawing of fruit became less flat.) When the patient again suggested destroying her design, the therapist reminded her that is was important to keep it. She was then for the first time given a psychological interpretation of her destructive impulse toward all her pictures. It was explained to her that she was turning her repressed anger on to her pictures instead of against herself.

Again, in this session, Mrs. Arnstein talked of her concern about money and stated that she feared she could not afford to continue the art therapy sessions indefinitely.

Fifth Session

In the fifth session the patient was shown how to use the scribble technique as a means of helping her to become more spontaneous in her expression. She made three attempts to use this method, but in some of the following pictures it was far from successful.

Fig. 58.   The Upright Plate of Fruit.

In a scribble drawing of a Woman's Torso (not shown), the patient emphasized the distinguishing feminine elements of the breasts but significantly avoided any suggestion of the woman's vulva, thus suggesting the patient's repression of her own sexuality since the death of her husband. At this time the patient began to resist the idea of continuing the use of the scribble technique. When asked why, she answered, "Because it's new." She did identify several forms within the loops as fruit and then called one "a fetus in the womb." To this fetus-like form she added a face and tail. Speculations and phantasies about pregnancy appeared again later in several of the patient's pictures. She said that she had hoped that she was pregnant when her husband died, and she had also drawn a picture of her dream about her murdered daughter in which she saw her as pregnant (Fig. 71).

Abstract Blue Pattern

When the patient's inhibitions made her unable to produce any further free-flowing designs with the scribble technique, she projected this angular and jagged blue-line pattern (Fig. 59). As she made her sudden and angry strokes, she was unaware of the degree of intense hostility and aggression that she was releasing. Again she wished to destroy this "awful" picture.

Bloody Hands

This painting of bloody hands (Fig. 60) was given to the therapist without any explanation on the day in which she also drew a picture about the murder of her family by the Nazis. No words were necessary.

Three Black Tombstones

Then Mrs. Arnstein did dare, in her drawing of the Three Black Tombstones (Fig. 61), to show for the first time her tragic grief about the murder of her family. She sat down and went right to work drawing this devastating picture of the black tombstones of her eldest daughter, her husband and their child. As she began to draw this picture, she asked, "How do you make a figure crucified?" But without waiting for an answer she drew the three black tombstones with crosses. It was strange that this Jewish woman placed crosses on these tombstones. Her inquiry may have involved the symbolic crucifixion of her family.

When she had finished this drawing, she pointed to the small head of a child that she had drawn opposite the tombstones and said, "I wonder whose head that is?" The patient and the therapist both knew that it was her dead grandchild.

A Second Picture of the Black Tombstones and Black Trees, Brightened with Rust-colored Blossoms

To complete the release of her sorrow about the loss of her family, the patient made this second drawing of the tombstones (Fig. 62). This time she drew three plain black tombstones with some black trees behind them. The intensity of feeling in this picture was reduced by the less heavy use of black and the addition of rust-colored blossoms to the trees and a bouquet of rust-colored flowers on a table beside the graves of her family. She made no comment but she had here symbolically expressed the lightening of her sorrow in this second, less somber drawing.

The Patient Develops Her Own Symbolic Pictorial Language

After Mrs. Arnstein began to express her long-repressed anguish in the Three Black Tombstones picture, she then found it possible to continue the release of her grief in many other pictures. In the next session the patient made two drawings of completely black jars—both wordless symbols of her deep depression.

Black Jar with Yellow Flower

In one of these black jars (Fig. 63) she placed a brilliant yellow flower. The introduction of this bright yellow flower against the black jar suggested, as did the addition of rust-colored flowers to the second Black Tombstone picture, that here too the patient's deep depression was lifting. Besides a repetitious drawing of black jars and black tree trunks, the patient began to draw figures of a woman, herself, always dressed in black. For sixteen years, since the

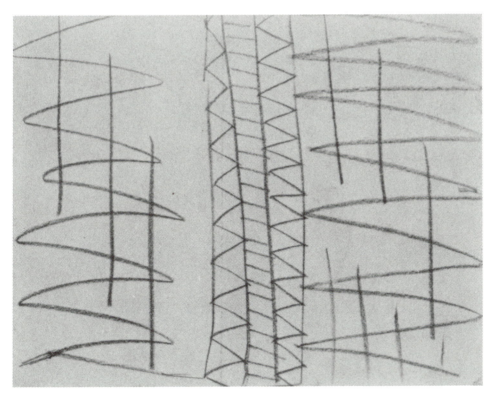

Fig. 59.   Abstract Blue Pattern.

death of her husband, the patient had always worn black. Only near the end of the therapy sessions did she buy herself a dark blue evening dress. This dress plays an important role in her later picture "The Dream of My Blue Evening Dress" (Fig. 76). Elated by the growth of her creative expression, the patient announced at the end of this session, "I don't want to be pretty and stupid, but intelligent and useful."

When in the sixth session the patient brought in a drawing of Lemons on a Plate (not shown), she was again angry at her inability to draw the plate in perspective. The best that could be done to help her with this picture was to show her how to reduce the flatness of the fruit by modeling the form of the lemons with the addition of shadows.

As the patient gained a deeper understanding of how to compose a picture and as she began to realize that the use of color could be controlled, she was able to voice her new realization that "there is no sense in rushing to finish a picture before you understand how to do it." At this time she was able to express a more positive attitude toward the art therapy sessions by saying, "How much I'm learning."

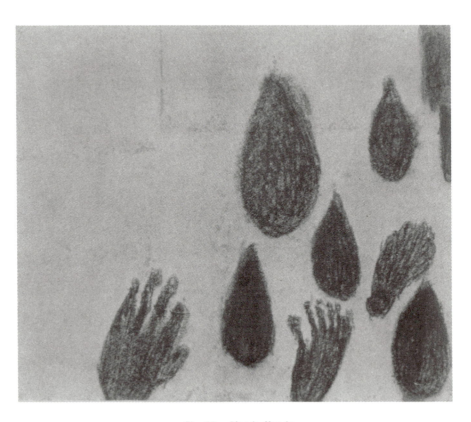

Fig. 60. Bloody Hands.

Fig. 61.   Three Black Tombstones.

Fig. 62.   A Second Picture of the Black Tombstones and Black Trees, Brightened with Rust-colored Blossoms.

Fig. 63.   Black Jar with Yellow Flower.

SERIES OF SELF-IMAGES

As Mrs. Arnstein's creative ability developed, she began to draw a number of symbolic self-images that were quite revealing.

The Patient Mourning with a Red Rose at the Tombstones of Her Dead Family

This romantic self-image of a virginal self, holding a rose as she mourns at the graves of her dead family (Fig. 64) was drawn twice by the patient. The psychoanalyst had told the art therapist, as well as Mrs. Arnstein, that she had dramatized her life in the virginal role.

A pencil sketch of a nude man and woman standing together beneath a tree (not shown) was called by the patient "Lost Love." It was evidently a romantic phantasy about her marriage and the loss of her husband through death.

A Phantasied Self-Portrait

Some weeks later the patient made this very different type of phantasied self-portrait in which she recalled her younger days (Fig. 65). There is some evidence of the influence of Modigliani, whose exhibition she had just seen.

"A Pregnant Woman"

This picture (Fig. 66) is again a repetition of the patient's obsession with pregnancy.

Pewter Picture with Autumn Leaves and Grapes

This more elaborate composition (Fig. 67) was begun at home and then reworked for several sessions with the therapist. The pewter pitcher had originally a flat, pale, slate-gray surface; the leaves were of the same unrelieved flatness as the jar, and the grapes were also drawn without any modeling. Dissatisfied with her uncontrolled efforts, the patient was now ready to work seriously instead of merely amusing herself. (Although she made no reference to the reappearance of a small woman's head in this design, it was surely herself again.)

The patient drew several pictures expressing her response to her recent trip to the country in the fall. When she showed them to the therapist, she was again very angry that she was unable to make the leaves on the lower part of the page, as she said, "lie down on the ground, as I know they should." Again she was baffled by the problem of perspective.

A Blue Table and Fruit

In this picture (Fig. 68), drawn at home, the patient's inability to apply her study of perspective is repeated. Her continuing rage against herself for her "childish" and "silly" drawings was a substitute for her rage against the emptiness of her own ego, which had replaced her grief at the death of both her husband and her daughter.

Freud, in his analysis of melancholia, offered a key to this patient's deep depression: "In grief the world becomes poor and empty; in melancholia it is the ego itself. The patient represents his ego to us as worthless, incapable of

Fig. 64. The Patient Mourning with a Red Rose at the Tombstones of Her Dead Family.

Fig. 65.   A Phantasied Self-Portrait.

our effort and morally despicable, he reproaches himself, vilifies himself and expects to be cast out and chastized."[1] This attitude of self-vilification toward herself is just what this depressed woman indulged in during the early art therapy sessions.

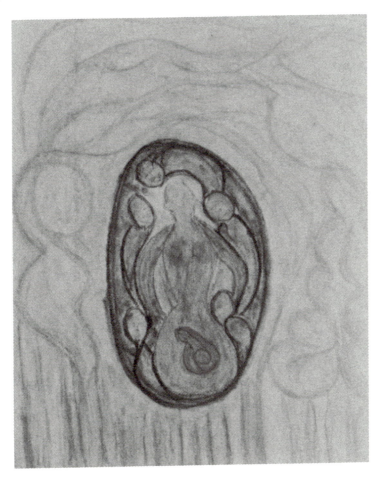

Fig. 66. "A Pregnant Woman."

Self-Image with Black Surround and Flower Spray

This drawing (Fig. 69) is of particular interest because it introduces the patient's use for the first time of a black surround on a figure which was herself. She now began to elaborate this form of a self-image in a number of her later large pictures which offered significant aspects of her past and present life.

[1] Freud, S.: "Mourning and Melancholia." *Collected Papers.* London, Hogarth Press and Institute of Psychoanalysis, 1956, Vol. IV, p. 155.

Fig. 67.   Pewter Picture with Autumn Leaves and Grapes.

Fig. 68.   A Blue Table and Fruit.

Fig. 69.   Self-Image with Black Surround and Flower Spray.

Vase of Gladiolas on a Stand

This lovely and sensitive drawing of gladiolas on a stand (Fig. 70) was drawn by the patient during an art therapy session. At this time she was consciously able to apply to the oval stand beneath the flowers what she had gained in her study of perspective. But when she had thus mastered the application of perspective in some of her drawings, such knowledge would suddenly slip from her consciousness and might disappear from her pictures for some time.

Fig. 70. Vase of Gladiolas on a Stand.

"Woman in a Golden Dress": First Dream

Mrs. Arnstein made this picture of her dream (Fig. 71) at home. Pointing to the form of the woman, she first spoke of the blood hue which showed in the picture; then she spoke of the child in the womb of the woman. The woman's figure, she said, recalled her daughter, slain by the Nazis. She had imagined the daughter as pregnant at the time of her death. Pointing again to the red line in the picture, she explained that this blood stream "goes from the child to the mother's heart." Then referring to the head of the woman, she explained, "The way the hair is drawn back flat is like yours." Continuing her associations to her dream picture, the patient said, "The golden color of the dress is like the color of the gold curtains here in your office." In her free associations to her dream picture, the patient had been able to verbalize clearly the development of her positive transference to the therapist.

"My Husband's Hand Reaching Down from Icy Mountains, and My Own Hand, Unable to Get Him": Second Dream

As Mrs. Arnstein described this second dream (Fig. 72), she said that in it she saw herself reaching upward toward her husband while he reached down toward her from the heights of the icy mountains. But in the dream she never reached him. When the therapist urged the patient to draw this dream, she said that she could not because she did not know how to draw hands. The therapist then offered to pose for her, first taking the position of the patient reaching her hand upward to her husband, and then reversing the arm position as if the husband were reaching downward toward the patient. Mrs. Arnstein tried to draw the hands in both positions. She then began to draw her entire dream by outlining the snow mountain and adding pine trees. She next drew her own hand reaching upward and her husband's hand reaching downward toward her hand.

The patient's ability to express the dream about her dead husband in a picture showed a great advance in her capacity to release her long-repressed suffering. This visualization of the accident which caused the husband's death, as well as the two tombstone pictures (Figs. 61 and 62), marked a positive development in the patient's response to therapy.

"A Mermaid"

The patient surprised the therapist at the next session by bringing in this large and imaginative design of a mermaid (Fig. 73) whose head is framed in long brown tresses as she reclines diagonally against a blue sea. In her lap she holds three small mermaid children, and the mermaid's eyes are blue like her own. There is an imaginative freedom in this composition, with its reddish purple grasses rising from the blue water and its school of blue fish forming a rhythmic pattern. Although the patient did not verbally identify the mermaid with herself, the number of children in the mermaid's lap is identical with the number of the patient's children.

Fig. 71.   "Woman in a Golden Dress": First Dream.

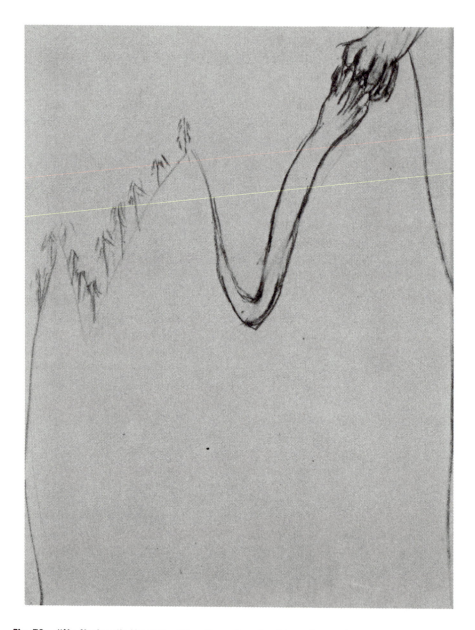

Fig. 72.   "My Husband's Hand Reaching Down from Icy Mountains, and My Own Hand, Unable to Get Him": Second Dream.

Practice Sketches

In order to make the patient more aware of actual subjects that could be studied for creating pictures, she was urged to turn her eyes toward the world around her. Considerable time was spent in encouraging the patient to make studies of real flowers, such as gladiolas (Fig. 70), bird of paradise flowers and peonies, instead of her imaginary pansies with faces. At one time it was suggested that she draw the scene from her window, which was her only effort at landscape.

The Patient's Pictures about Herself

In the seventh month of therapy, Mrs. Arnstein made an impressive series of large pictures which dealt with herself in relation to her entire life cycle. These designs show a dramatic development in the patient's art expression, which led to a growing insight about herself and the purpose of art therapy.

"A Woman and a Tree: Eternity for Me"

This figure of a nude woman (Fig. 74) shows a new bold effort on the part of the patient which directly inspired the next design.

"Four Generations: Eternity and Suffering"

In this beautifully composed and rhythmic design, called by the patient "Four Generations: Eternity and Suffering" (Fig. 75, used as Frontispiece), she explained that the figures of the three women begin at the left of the picture with her mother, then herself, followed by her daughter and her grandson. She said that in this picture, contrary to the previous one, she had remembered to put the hearts on the left side of each body where they belonged.

Fig. 73. "A Mermaid." Color plate on page xx.

"The Dream of My Blue Evening Dress": Made after Seeing the Play "The Rose Tattoo"

This unusually complex design (Fig. 76) was made by Mrs. Arnstein on the evening when she had seen Tennessee Williams' play, "The Rose Tattoo." It was, she explained, a picture that combined her response to this play and her recollection of a recent dream about her new blue evening dress. The therapist had not seen the play and wanted to know how the picture was related to the play. As the patient began to explain the story of the play, her eyes filled with tears. The plot, she explained, dealt with the life of a widowed Sicilian peasant woman whose husband had been killed in an accident. This woman, the patient continued, had preserved her husband's ashes upon an altar with an ever-burning light. Two women friends of this Sicilian widow had visited her in one important scene of the play and asked her why she was grieving for a husband who had been unfaithful to her. The peasant woman, when convinced by her friends that her husband had not been true to her, broke the container of the husband's ashes (which she had kept in her home) and then extinguished the light that she had always kept burning beside it.

When the patient was asked by the therapist why she had been so moved by the play, she replied with reluctance that one of her women friends had visited her after her husband's death and had told her that people were saying his death was really a suicide, not a ski accident as had originally been reported. The patient then emphasized to the therapist that never before had she told this to anyone. There was no doubt that seeing the play had brought back the patient's repressed and painful memory that her long-idealized marriage might not have been as perfect as she claimed.

When the patient was asked to explain the various parts of this complex design, she began by pointing to the dominant figure of the radiant young woman in the blue evening dress. This, she said, was herself.

What is striking about the self portrait is that the patient had pictured herself as a much younger woman—closer to the age of the widow in the play and closer to the age when she herself had been widowed. In the drawing the patient had placed a large, bright flower in her hair, which (the therapist noticed when she went to see the play the next day) was identical with the flower worn by the Sicilian widow. The gaudy red and black jewelry which the patient wore in this picture was also quite unlike her ladylike taste.

The patient drew herself wearing one black and one red earring and the necklace is also divided with one side red and one side black, but she gave no explanation of why she had done this. Perhaps in the color contrast of the red and black she was symbolizing her divided self, the black part representing mourning and the red raising doubts about her husband's faithfulness.

The patient had been too disturbed by her experience at the play to say more about her picture on this day, but at the following session she was ready, when asked, to explain the different elements of the picture. First, she explained that she had drawn herself in this new blue evening dress because she had just then recalled it from a forgotten dream. The association of the patient's first non-

Fig. 74.   "A Woman and a Tree: Eternity for Me."

black dress, purchased after fifteen years of mourning her dead husband, drama-tized the question which the play had unconsciously released in her—whether she should or should not have mourned her husband all those years.

The many symbolic elements of this picture were complex. Besides drawing herself in the blue evening dress, the patient pointed to the fragmented parts of the same blue dress and her separated head in the lower right corner of the picture. The blue dress and herself within it, she said, had been torn apart by her mother. This image represented, openly and for the first time, her deep resentment against the mother. The patient then pointed to the two faces that she had drawn within her own bent arms in the central figure of herself. Within the left arm, she explained, was the black and threatening head of the mother and within the right arm was the face of the therapist. There was no doubt that this symbolic opposition of the two heads represented the patient's hostility to her "bad" mother and her growing transference to the therapist as the "good" mother.

The patient then drew attention to the black arch in the upper left-hand corner of her picture and said that it stood for the black shadows of hate and unhappiness of her early childhood, and below the arch is the mother's head. But the three lighted candles within the black archway, she added, stood for the promise of faith and hope in childhood. This symbolic recall of her early years led the patient to admit for the first time the extent of her mother's lack of understanding or sympathy for her. She then suddenly recalled how her mother had demanded, when she was a child, to see a poem that she was hiding in her pocket. When the patient, unwilling to expose her poem, denied that she had hidden it, the mother had accused her of both lying and stupidity.

The therapist then asked her to explain the black outline figure in the lower left corner of the picture, and the patient said that it was herself. Then, smiling knowingly, she added, "I have no eyes to see in this drawing." She then asked rhetorically, "Who can this head of the man be?" She was referring to the large face inside a heart outline which she had drawn within her own body. "Could it be my husband?" she continued. But then she added, "Maybe it's Christ. . . . That makes me think again of 'The Rose Tattoo' play where the peasant woman worshipped her husband's ashes beside a Catholic shrine with a figure of Christ." (Here again is the patient's identification with the unhappy Sicilian peasant widow.)

In the lower right-hand corner the patient had drawn a tiny picture of the grandson who had already appeared in the drawing "Four Generations" (Fig. 75).

In the creation of this picture, Mrs. Arnstein had revealed in her symbolic images many of her unconscious conflicts that she had as yet been unable to express in words during the art therapy sessions. These new realizations included her admission of doubts about the cause of her husband's death and her pre-viously unvoiced hostility against her mother, as well as a pictorial expression of her transference to the therapist as a "good" mother in contrast to her own mother as "bad." The patient had also drawn in this picture the oral incorpora-

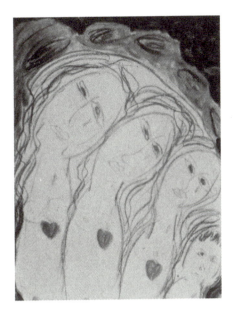

Fig. 75. "Four Generations: Eternity and Suffering." Color plate on page xxiv.

Fig. 76. "The Dream of My Blue Evening Dress": Made after Seeing the Play "The Rose Tattoo." Color plate on page xix.

tion of her husband within her own body. This typical response of a depressed patient is well described by Fenichel: "Depression is a desperate attempt to compel an orally incorporated object [in this case we know it was the patient's husband] to grant forgiveness, protection, love and security."[2]

Before Mrs. Arnstein had been able to work through the "free associations" to this complex picture, she had seen no therapeutic value in the process of art therapy as a means of uncovering her repressed conflicts. Now, however, for the first time the patient said that she was convinced that her pictures could say things before she could put them into words.

"The Hat: My Feelings about My Sister"

In the seventh month of art therapy, Mrs. Arnstein was able in this picture (Fig. 77) to express for the first time her long-repressed resistance against her older sister. She called this drawing "The Hat: My Feelings About My Sister." It was drawn three days after the picture of the Blue Evening Dress. "My sister," explained the patient, "arrived from Europe with ten hats and no money. That's why I drew this picture."

The patient has drawn her sister flaunting a gay flowered hat, while she has pictured herself, again with a virginal air, as enveloped in the mourning of a black surround. Glancing at this picture, the patient told the therapist, "I'm ashamed to see that I made myself so fine and my sister so mean." In this comment the patient revealed her sense of guilt at having contrasted her own other-worldliness to her sister's frivolity. The patient then enlarged on her disapproval of her sister's moral laxness and financial irresponsibility, but then she admitted that she envied her sister's easygoing disposition and wished that she herself worried less about her own financial security.

When the sister visited the patient again, Mrs. Arnstein discovered that she was now able for the first time in her life to block her sister's attempts to pry into her personal affairs. She stopped her sister's efforts to investigate her psychotherapy by locking her drawers and her closet so that her sister could not see either her notes or her drawings.

Mrs. Arnstein then declared, "I now see my sister in a new light; she talks only about herself and never listens to what I have to say. She keeps telling me about all the men who are interested in her." A few days later the patient added, "I am different from my sister. She has a happier disposition. I know that with my nature, I would not live life in her way."

"Myself, My Children and My Grandchild"

In this picture, which the patient called "Myself, My Children and My Grandchild" (Fig. 78), she is continuing to review her past and present family life. Here she has again drawn herself with a heavy black surround. She holds a tiny baby in her arms and to her left she has drawn her daughter, her son-in-law and their small child.

---

[2] Fenichel, O.: *The Psychoanalytic Theory of the Neuroses.* New York, W. W. Norton, 1945, p. 396.

Fig. 77.   "The Hat: My Feelings about my Sister."
Color plate on page xx.

Fig. 78.   "Myself, My Children and My Grandchild." Color plate on page xxii.

When the therapist asked the patient about the baby she was holding in her arms, she said, "When my husband died, I kept hoping that I was pregnant, for I wanted another child so much." The patient had previously projected this same wish of pregnancy onto her dead daughter in her drawing "Woman in a Golden Dress" (Fig. 71). In this picture, the patient had drawn, as in a previous one, a thin red line that linked the grandchild directly to the figure of the patient. When she was asked its meaning, she said, "It's the bloodstream to your own child through the grandchild. That's very important."

That the creation of this family picture was stimulated by the patient's most recent session with the psychoanalyst became evident as she told of her talk with him. "It was easier now to talk more with Dr. L. I did very good advances in a good direction with him yesterday. This picture shows now I must grow up; it shows the problem how I must separate myself from my children. The picture of myself is drawn so severe and cold." The analyst had been trying to make the patient aware for some time of her overattachment to her daughter and her family. She was now for the first time beginning to face this problem. Mrs. Arnstein then remarked, "I always feel better at my daughter's when her husband is away working. When he's home I feel too much there. They all kiss each other all the time. Dr. L. says my feelings—it's jealousy. God forbid, I'm jealous! My daughter she loves him [meaning her husband]. He has no money. She has to sacrifice so much. But I am glad they are happy together."

As she continued to examine her drawing, she reminisced about her daughter as a child. "Frieda was only three," she explained, "when her father died, and she always wanted more affection. My kisses she would often say were not warm enough."

"Myself as a Child: My Father and Myself Grown Up"

This large drawing (Fig. 79) was the last in the group of pictures covering the patient's family cycle. This series of pictures, which began with "Four Generations" (Fig. 75), was created during a period of two weeks. This final two-part picture was called by the patient "Myself as a Child: My Father and Myself Grown Up." Mrs. Arnstein explained that this picture represented herself in two stages of her life, both as a child and as a grown-up woman. As this cycle of family pictures had evolved, the patient was surprised to find that she was able to recall many forgotten memories of happy and unhappy experiences in both her childhood and adult years.

Only by questioning the patient about the significance of each figure in this picture did its symbolic meaning become clear. When asked about the figure of the tall, gray-bearded man in the center of her design, the patient said, "It resembles my father. I wanted to make him a little like Lincoln. I wanted to make him a great man. But it's so childish." Again the therapist assured the patient that she had created an important picture of personal significance in which she had been able to express effectively both her memories and feelings in a way that achieved the true purpose of art therapy.

When the therapist pointed to the child holding a bouquet, the patient said, "It's me as a little girl. See the three yellow candles behind me. It's like in that other picture of 'The Blue Evening Dress' (Fig. 76). The three candles always show the happiness of childhood, always show the light, seeing good things. You know how today I am happy with just the little things."

As the patient continued to gaze at this picture about herself as a child, memories of her early years came back to her. "I always wanted to be a mother, when I was young," she said. "My sister was always interested in books. I always played with dolls. These dolls were already my children. When I was fourteen I was still fond of dolls. But you cannot have a doll at that age. I always played with dolls. They were real children to me. I hid them from my mother. Even when I was eighteen, I hid a doll in my closet. During all those years when I was first married, with my children around me, I always felt good. My feeling about my children was the same as with the dolls. I had forgotten all about it, until now as I made this picture."

Turning from the part of the drawing of herself as a child, Mrs. Arnstein then considered her self-portrait as a mature woman. She pointed to the way that she had drawn the faces of her three children as coming out of her head. Asked why she had placed them there, she questioned, "Why do they come out of my head?" Urged to answer her own question, she said, "Because my children are brain children. They came when we planned them."

"I think," she explained "that in this drawing of myself grown up, I've made myself very hard—with something very mean about myself. I thought to myself as I drew it, 'Now don't make it like a madonna.'" She explained she was here referring to the psychoanalyst's repeated comments to her about her concept of herself as a virginal figure—like the ones she had drawn of herself holding a rose. The analyst had said, she explained in her awkward English, that "I did not wish to be disflowered."

Fig. 79. "Myself as a Child: My Father and Myself Grown Up." Color plate on page xxiii.

There were several symbolic aspects of this picture which needed further clarification. The patient was therefore asked about the faces that were drawn within the heart-shape outlines of both her father's and her own adult body. "The face drawn inside of my father is my mother," she explained. "Father and Mother loved each other very much. I believe that she wanted to die after he did. She died a year later of cancer. I always took care of her. My sister couldn't stand being near her then. She had changed so much. The picture inside the heart shape in the drawing of my grown-up self is, of course, my husband."

The patient had also in this picture drawn a red line between the figures, which she had described as the blood-tie that joined generations (Fig. 78). She did not, however, elaborate concerning the same red blood line of this picture, which connected herself as a child to the heart of the father and then continued into the heart of her adult self.

The Patient Shows Her Pictures to the Psychoanalyst

In spite of her constant protest to the therapist that her pictures were "childish," she had begun to realize that her pictures were important enough to show to the psychoanalyst. When she told the art therapist that she had shown her recent pictures to him, she explained, "I didn't want to do it, because they are so bad, but I showed the pictures to Dr. L. anyway." When she was asked by the art therapist about the analyst's response, she said, "He found my pictures interesting." But then, still feeling the need to belittle herself, she added with a touch of her original arrogance, "I'm amazed that it took me so long, seven months, to get so far."

"Myself with All the Men Staring at Me"

After completing the family cycle, Mrs. Arnstein had drawn this final revealing self-portrait (Fig. 80). In this design she has returned again to her virginal self-image holding a rose. Against a deep blue background she had placed the sexually aggressive males that she has always feared.

Bowl of Peonies

This was one of several studies of peonies made by the patient after her month's absence on a vacation cruise (Fig. 81). It shows that the patient had developed considerable competence and sensitivity in making an objective study.

The Patient Tries Going to an Art School

When the patient was leaving to spend the summer with her daughter in the country, she announced her intention of going to a class in a nearby art school to help her to improve her art expression. Although the art therapist did nothing to discourage the patient's decision, she did not anticipate any positive results. She was therefore not surprised to be told later by the patient that the summer art class had been too difficult, so she dropped out. But undaunted by this defeat, the patient announced to the therapist in the fall that she had signed

Fig. 80. "Myself with All the Men Staring at Me."

Fig. 81.   Bowl of Peonies.

up for a sculpture class at a university and a painting class at The Museum of Modern Art.

The patient was then reminded by the art therapist that in the previous spring, when she had spoken of her intention to go to some regular art classes, she had been told that if she went for art lessons, she must drop the art therapy sessions. Mrs. Arnstein refused to see why the two approaches were incompatible. In order to clarify the issue, the art therapist had asked the psychoanalyst to meet with the patient and herself to review this question. At the conference, the psychoanalyst supported the art therapist's point of view, but the patient still refused to accept the idea that the art therapy sessions and the art lessons could not continue simultaneously. As the patient and art therapist left the analyst's office, Mrs. Arnstein asked the art therapist whether she might still see her, once in a while, even though she went to the art classes. This was readily agreed to and a friendly contact has continued up to the present time.

The patient was eager to show the art therapist some of her small sculpture figures made during that fall. They were quite without personal quality, and the sculpture class did not stimulate the patient to continue beyond a single term.

Mrs. Arnstein's report on the result of her first painting class, however, showed her surprise when her composition was singled out by her art instructor as the best in the class. This experience gave the patient some proof that she had learned about creative art expression from her art therapy sessions, but the patient's interest in developing her own art expression dwindled away before the end of the year and she soon dropped out of both art classes.

The art therapist has been able to keep up a friendly contact with this patient and was pleased to learn that the patient had freed herself from her overattachment to the daughter and her child. She also heard that having overcome her previous anxiety Mrs. Arnstein was now able to travel freely with friends to such distant places as Europe and Mexico.

The patient had stopped seeing the psychoanalyst and had become well-adjusted to living alone. She had also succeeded in building up an interesting personal life for herself which now extended beyond her immediate family. She told the art therapist, with a smile, that on her sister's last visit from abroad she had made it quite clear to her sister that she no longer intended to be bossed by her. Then she added proudly, "My sister accepted my new independence."

Another proof of the patient's recovery was given to the therapist when Mrs. Arnstein declared, "You know, until now that I am well, I had no idea how sick I was when I came to you."

INDEX

Alexander, F., 44
Appel, K. E., 31
Arp, J., 46
Art, spontaneous
  method of introduction to patients, 7
  when created, 7
Art materials, 15
Art teaching *vs.* art therapy, 14-15
Artist, professional, 15, 18
  case study of, 49-84
  treatment of, 4

Bader, A., 23-24
Behlen, F., 14
Berger, L. F., 10, 11-12
Bildnerei der Geisteskranken (Prinzhorn), 22-23
Black, use of in depression, 9
Bychowski, G., 19

Caldwell, J., 12
Case studies, 48-165
  alcoholic patient, 85-127
  depressed patient, 129-165
  ulcer patient, 49-84
"Case Studies of Pupils or Patients Blocked in Creative Expression," 35-36
Change, symbolic expression of, 9
Christianity and sexual symbols, 40-42
Creative ability, recovery of, 18

Definition of art therapy, 1-4
Depressed patients
  case history, 129-165
  use of black, 9
Development of art therapy in U.S.A., 31-36
Diagnostic value, 8-10
Drawing tests *vs.* art therapy, 9-10

European approach to art therapy, 22-25
  see also "Symbolic realization"; "Symbolic painting"
Evolution of art therapy, 30-31

Family therapy, 10-11
Frequency of sessions, 8
Freud, S., 2, 3, 8, 21-22, 24, 28, 33, 39, 40, 44-45
  see also Freudian psychoanalysis
Freudian psychoanalysis, 3
Freudian psychoanalysis *vs.* dynamically oriented art therapy, 16-21
Fry, R., 40

Giedion, S., 37-39, 46, 47
Group therapy, 10-13

Hohepa Te Rake, 43
Holt, R. H., 29
Huxley, A., 29

Impressionism, 44
Inman, T., 40-42
Interviewing, 35
  technique, 34

Jones, E., 28
Jung, C., 21-22, 24, 33
  see also Jungian analytic psychology
Jungian analytic psychology, 3
Jungian analytic psychology *vs.* art therapy, 21-22

Kinesthetic perceptions, 18
Knight, P., 40
Kris, E., 21
Kwiafkowska, H. Y., 10-11

Length of sessions, 7-8
Lewis, N. P. C., 30-31
Luquet, 40, 44

Malraux, A., 42, 45
May, R., 21
Meares, A., 26, 27-28
Motivation to seek art therapy, 4-6

Obese women, art therapy of, 12-13
Occupational therapy, 10, 25
 vs. art therapy, 13-14

Paranoid images, 9
Plokker, J. H., 23, 24-25
Polatin, P., 31
Progressive aspect of symbols, 21
Psychologists, clinical, art therapy course
 for, 36

Rabinovitch, R., 5-6
Red and black, use of to express hatred
 of parent, 21
Regression in art expression, 21
Repression
 and symbolism, 29
Rout, E. A., 43

Schizophrenia, 8-9, 22-28
Schizophrenic images, 8-9
"Scribble" technique, 15-16, 17, 33
Sculpture, 7, 14

Sechehaye, M. A., 26-27
Simon, M. P., 45
Spider, as symbol of mother, 21
Spitz, R., 16-18
Steck, H., 24
Stern, M. M., 19-21
Suitability of art therapy, 6
Symbol, power of, 36-47
"Symbolic painting," 27-28
"Symbolic realization," 26-27
Symbolism, psychoanalytic definition of,
 29
Symbolism as nonverbal expression, 25-30

Technique, 6-7
Therapist, training of, 14
Training in art therapy, 31-36
Training of art therapist, 5
Transference, 2, 6
 in art therapy vs. psychoanalysis, 17-18
 importance of, 8
Transparency, 44, 45, 46-47
 in primeval art, 39

Ulcer patients, 9
 case history, 49-84

Verbalization, 3-4
 expansion through art therapy, 7

Wilder, J., 11
Wynne, L., 10-11